# Rise of the Cyber Women
# Volume III

Lisa Ventura MBE

February 29, 2024

First printing 2024 1 3 5 7 9 10 8 6 4 2

978-1-7385153-3-2

Security Blend Books

https://securityblendbooks.com

*This book is dedicated to all the women in the cyber security industry who work tirelessly to combat the growing cyber threat, today and every day.*

# Acknowledgements and Thanks

I would like to thank all the incredible women in cyber security who are featured in this book for taking the time to complete the interview questions to give readers an insight into their career pathways, and how they got where they are today in the industry.

I would also like to thank James Bore of Security Blend Books, not only for publishing this collection of interviews, but for his unwavering help and support to me in the time that I've been in the industry.

Finally, I'd like to thank my long-suffering husband Russell Ventura for always believing in me and supporting me with what I do. I know how hard it is to live with me and my neurodivergent conditions of autism and ADHD; he deserves a medal for making it this far with me.

# Foreword

I've known Lisa for a while now as a driven and active campaigner for diversity of all kinds in cyber security, among other things. A passionate advocate against bullying and for awareness of impostor syndrome, she tirelessly works to make the industry better both for those within it and the people we seek to defend. She also has excellent taste in comedy films. I'm honoured to count her as a friend, and was delighted when she asked me to write this foreword.

The Rise of the Cyber Women series has worked to highlight the diversity of women working in the cyber security industry ever since the first volume, and it's something that is very much needed. Despite some progress being made since the release of the first book in 2020 we have a very long way to go and highlighting the range of voices which make up the industry helps to continue in the right direction. Estimates of the proportion of women within cyber security vary and depend on a number of factors, including that defining the boundaries of the industry can be gently described as challenging, and run from anywhere from 10-30%. That's a long way from where it should be given the universality of the need for security.

Security threats, cyber or otherwise, do not discriminate in their attacks and as an industry our purpose is to protect people from these threats. We can best do that with as many different viewpoints, ways of thinking, and experiences as possible. When we only have one set of similar experiences to draw from we fail to even see some of the risks that will impact us and others, let alone mitigate against them in any effective way. This series is about more than just sharing advice on getting into the industry and examples of the different routes, it showcases the varied experiences that are so vital to understanding the threats and defences out there.

Lisa embodies the spirit of what the Rise of the Cyber Women series aims to achieve: showcasing not just the achievements but also the ongoing challenges faced by women in the cyber security field. Her dedication to working towards an inclusive environment where diverse voices are heard and valued is a testament to her character and her commitment to the industry. Through her work, Lisa has not only contributed to the field, she has also paved the way for future generations of cyber professionals, especially women, to find their place and thrive.

In this volume, you will find stories that are both inspiring and eye-opening. Each contributor has shared their unique journey, shedding light on the obstacles they've overcome, the successes they've achieved, the lessons they've learned along the way, and the advice they have to share with others. These interviews are not just about the technical aspects of working in cyber security but are deeply personal accounts that highlight the resilience, determination, and passion required to excel in this field.

You will see in many of these stories reminders of the importance of mentorship, community, and support in fostering diversity and inclusion within cyber security. It is through listening to and learning from each other's experiences that we can continue to break down barriers and build a more inclusive industry. And it is incumbent on those of us established in the industry to provide a boost to those looking to enter and grow within it.

This volume of The Rise of the Cyber Women will not only serve as a source of inspiration for those considering a career in cyber security but also provide a call to action for everyone within the industry to play their part in promoting diversity and inclusion. We should all take a lesson from Lisa's book (the metaphorical one, not one of the physical ones, I don't support damage to books) and work to make the cyber security world a place where everyone feels welcome, valued, and empowered to contribute to our collective security.

I am grateful to Lisa for the opportunity to contribute to this important work and look forward to seeing the continued impact of The Rise of the Cyber Women series in promoting diversity and inclusion in cyber security.

- James Bore CSyP

# Introduction

Introduction It is 2024, and we are still talking about the cyber skills gap and how we can attract more women into cyber security. I was having these conversations with organizations over ten years ago, and while the careers landscape has improved for women in the industry in that time, there still remains a large skills gap and a lack of women in cyber security.

According to the UK Government report "Cyber security skills in the UK Labour market[1]" which was released in 2023, only 17% of the cyber sector workforce is female, a number that is down from 22% in 2022. In addition, only 14% of senior roles are filled by women. It is clear that although progress is being made, there is still much to be done to attract more women into the cyber security industry.

I first had the idea for "The Rise of the Cyber Women" back in 2020. The global pandemic was at its height, and we were all in lockdown. I wanted to shine a light on some of the amazing women in cyber security, talk about the incredible work they do and hopefully inspire the next gen-

---

[1] https://www.gov.uk/government/publications/cyber-security-skills-in-the-uk-labour-market-2023

eration to consider a career in cyber security. The goal of
the book was for readers to think, "wow, I could do that"
when they read the book and be inspired to get into cyber
security.

I also wanted to dispel many of the myths that exist for
women in cyber security today, and getting into the industry generally, such as:

### *You need a degree to get into cyber security*

This is simply not true, there are many other pathways
into the industry. You might decide to do a cyber security
skills bootcamp, such as the brilliant one offered today
by Capslock[2], or take some certifications in cyber security
that you are most interested in. I did not go down the
degree pathway, at the time that I could have gone to
University I backed out of going to stay at home and look
after my father who was in ill health at the time in the
early 1990s. I don't regret that decision, as I didn't get
saddled with a lot of student debt which many of my peers
had, and it hasn't impacted my career pathway in cyber
security one bit.

### *Cyber security is a male-dominated field; women are not welcome*

While it is true that women are underrepresented in cyber security, the industry is evolving, and efforts are being
made to create more inclusive environments. Many organizations actively seek to diversify their workforce and recognize the value of a gender-balanced team.

### *Women lack the technical skills required for cyber security roles*

---

[2]https://capslock.ac

Women possess the technical aptitude necessary for cyber-security roles. Many women excel in STEM fields and bring diverse perspectives that contribute to effective problem-solving and innovation. Encouraging and providing opportunities for skill development can help bridge any perceived gaps. I myself did not come from a technical background, and neither did some of the incredible and inspiring women showcased in this book.

*Women are not interested in cybersecurity.*

Interest in cyber security is not gender specific. Women, like men, have a keen interest in technology, problem-solving, and securing digital assets. Encouraging early exposure, mentorship, and awareness initiatives can help break down stereotypes and inspire women to pursue cyber security careers.

*Women in cyber security are more likely to face discrimination and hostility*

While I can say that this is true to some degree having experienced significant bullying and abuse in the cyber security industry, I have also had the support of many leading people in the industry too. For all the bullies and abusers that I encountered, there are many, many more incredible people in the cyber security industry who are only too happy to help and who are only a message or email away, and for that I am extremely grateful.

Due to the bullying and abuse I experienced in July 2021 which led me to considering coming out of the industry altogether, I didn't have the impetus to put together volume 3 of "The Rise of the Cyber Women" until now. Trauma runs deep, and having experienced bullying and abuse throughout my lifetime, I worked on addressing the root cause of it. This led me to becoming an expert in narcissism and narcissistic personality disorder, and how to handle these personality types on a personal and professional level. Whatever has happened to me, I always learn from the experience and give back as much as I can by supporting those who are also going through similar things to what I experienced.

While challenges still exist, the cyber security industry is actively working to address gender bias, discrimination and combat bullying and abuse. Organizations such as Respect in Security now exist, and many organizations are implementing policies to foster inclusivity and diversity. Supportive communities and networks also play a crucial role in helping women navigate and overcome challenges.

I hope that this book goes some small way to dispelling some of these myths, and I hope you all enjoy reading the interviews with all the incredible women in cyber security who are featured in this book as much as I enjoyed compiling it. I also hope it goes some small way to inspiring more women to consider cyber security as a rewarding career choice. I'm always open to a conversation around women in cyber, diversity in cyber security, neurodiversity or other key topics from the cyber security industry, so please email me via lisa@csu.org.uk if you would like to talk.

- Lisa Ventura MBE Founder: Cyber Security Unity

# Contents

Acknowledgements and Thanks      iii

Foreword      v

Introduction      ix

1   Dr Anmol Agarwal      1

2   Saja Aljulaud      11

3   Gabrielle Botbol      23

4   Emily Bridge      31

5   Rebecca Caldwell      37

6   Jan Carroll      43

7   Dr Andrea Cullen                        51

8   Eleanor Dallaway                        57

9   Deanna Gibb                             63

10 Laurie Gibbett                           71

11 Wendy Goucher                           75

12 Ellen Hallam                             79

13 Amelia Hewitt                            89

14 Bishakha Jain                            97

15 Bandana Kaur                            103

16 Sarah Knowles                           113

17 Amy Lewis                               119

18 Jacqui Loustau                          129

19 Emma Mackenzie                          137

20 Jelena Z. Matone                          141

21 Abigail McAlpine                          149

22 Connie McIntosh                           163

23 Hazel McPherson                           167

24 Elga Ximena Cardozo Moreno                173

25 Sarah Norman-Clarke                       179

26 Dr Ifeoma E. Nwafor                       183

27 Dooshima Dapo-Oyewole                     189

28 Stephanie Lynch-Ozanar                    195

29 Valerie Perlowitz                         203

30 Drenusha Salihu                           211

31 Caitlin Sauza                             221

32 Shifali Sharma                            227

**33 Dr Carrine Teoh Chooi Shi**      **233**

**34 Charlotte Smith**      **237**

**35 Rebecca Taylor**      **243**

**36 Andrea Themistou**      **253**

**37 Eleanor (Ellie) Upson**      **259**

**38 Ismini Vasileiou**      **265**

# Dr Anmol Agarwal

**Job Title:** Senior Security Researcher & Adjunct Professor

**Company/Organisation:** Nokia & George Washington University

*Tell us a bit about your background, your career to date and what you currently do in cyber security.*

I currently work as a senior security researcher at Nokia where I look at mitigating potential security vulnerabilities in technologies used in telecommunications networks like 5G and 6G. One of the main research areas I work on is looking at securing AI and Machine Learning. In 5G and 6G telecommunications networks, we might use AI features to harness more innovation. One big topic being talked about right now is the idea of using AI in 6G to optimize networks and having an AI native air interface. The AI technology will add new features to 6G, and my job is to secure these AI and Machine Learning technologies being used in 5G and 6G from being attacked. I work on a team whose job it is to analyse potential security vulnerabilities that could exist in new features proposed in 5G Advanced (the newer version of 5G) and 6G. I combine my background in AI, Machine Learning, and security in my job.

I'm also a part-time adjunct professor at the George Washington University in the School of Engineering and Applied Science. I'm currently teaching a doctoral machine learning course on Saturdays. The department also has cybersecurity courses as well.

I have a doctoral degree in cybersecurity analytics from George Washington University, and my research was focused on looking at adversarial machine learning attacks in Federated Learning. I studied how Machine Learning models respond when they are attacked. I also have a master's degree in computer science and a bachelor's degree in software engineering with an information assurance (cybersecurity) specialization from the University of Texas at Dallas.

*How did you get into the field of cyber security?*

I thought I was going to be a software developer like most of my peers, but I was inspired to pursue cybersecurity after my internship. During my internship, there was an insightful seminar that explained the importance of secure coding practices to software developers.

When I was an intern, I was working with a team of software engineers and was coding and deploying features on a real application that was used by the company in production. We followed an agile methodology approach, so all software developers worked in a very close-knit team. Because we were working on company cloud and web, it was also important to follow secure coding practices in our environment. Therefore, over the summer, the in-house security engineer provided security awareness training to encourage software developers to follow secure coding practices and to not be victims of common security attacks like SQL injection attacks or phishing emails. When the security engineer was demonstrating the different attacks, I was impressed that an SQL injection attack could be performed so easily, and because of that seminar, I was inspired to pursue cybersecurity. I understood that security was very important, and I was shocked at how sometimes, it could be so easy for a malicious person to attack a website or database. After my internship, I took a wide variety of cybersecurity and information security courses in graduate school to learn more about the field: data and applications security, information security, cloud security, and network security. With each course, I gained more knowledge about cybersecurity, and the courses I took in graduate school prepared me for my future cybersecurity career.

*What are the main challenges you've encountered as a woman in cyber security, and how did you overcome them?*

As a woman in cybersecurity, I've frequently been the only woman in the room whether in academic or professional settings. It was easy to feel left out initially, but I have found friends in the cybersecurity community which helped reduce my feelings of isolation. I joined outreach organizations like Women in CyberSecurity (WiCyS) and various local and online meetups for women in technology and cybersecurity professionals. Building my own network and finding friends within professional organizations has helped me feel like I belong in the community.

*What are the things you've learned being a woman in the cyber security industry?*

The cybersecurity field can be challenging as technology rapidly evolves. We constantly need to keep learning new things to ensure that we are up to date on the latest trends. It helps to be involved with meetups to discuss technology and cybersecurity news with peers, and there are many women in tech groups that also encourage women to network and share their own perspectives. As a woman in the industry, I have found that getting other mentors who have been through similar experiences has been very helpful. I have leaned on many of my mentors for support when encountering challenges. There are many outreach organizations that provide mentoring programs. I have been a mentor for Women in CyberSecurity (WiCyS) and Women of Color Advancing Peace, Security, and Conflict Transformation (WCAPS).

*What advice would you give to women who would like to join the cyber security industry?*

Follow your passion! If cybersecurity is something that interests you, go for it. Follow your interests and don't care what other people think.

I would also tell other women to not be intimidated by the portrayals in the media; not everyone in the cybersecurity field needs to be a hacker. You can be an ethical hacker if you're interested in that role, but there are so many other career options within the cybersecurity field. Cybersecurity will benefit from different perspectives and skillsets. Some potential careers in cybersecurity are being on the blue team (defensive side) in a role like a SOC (Security Operations Centre) analyst, purple team (both red or offensive and blue or defensive roles combined), design and development work, forensics, and analysis work. I would also tell women and others starting out in cybersecurity that you do not necessarily have to be what is traditionally known as "technical" and program/script things to have a successful career in cybersecurity. Roles in governance, risk, and compliance (GRC) are great and are needed in the industry; for example, right now, there is so much focus on GRC for AI to ensure that we are using AI responsibly and securely.

Explore all these different career paths in cybersecurity and analyse what you think you are interested in and would enjoy working on. Keep an open mind and be open to different types of roles. You might have always thought you wanted to be an ethical hacker on the red team side, but later, maybe you might change your mind and decide to be on the defensive blue team side. That's okay. It is okay to change your interests and to craft your own career path. Do not feel pressured to follow the exact footsteps of someone else because we all have our own strengths, and we might all have very different career paths in cybersecurity. Enjoy the journey!

*What role does diversity play in cyber security?*

Diversity is very important in cybersecurity. We need diverse teams to be able to solve challenging problems. By looking at a problem using multiple perspectives, we are more likely to arrive at innovative solutions.

I remember reading that studies have shown that diverse teams outperform other teams, tend to make less errors and make more money. Diversity is especially important in the cybersecurity context because a lot of the time, the attacks we face come from all over the world and are executed by people of various nationalities, backgrounds, and cultures. We should have a team of defenders that is also diverse so that we are better prepared to defend against different types of attacks.

To ensure that we attack diverse talent, it's important to show other young women – especially young women who identify as being a representative of a minority – that they too have a place in cybersecurity. We need more role models in the field to show them that they can also succeed in the field, which is why I'm so happy to contribute to this book. I also hope that more companies have outreach events to recruit more women and other minorities into cybersecurity careers. I obtained some of my career opportunities by simply attending a university networking event; without attending those events, I might have not even thought to apply or try to pursue that opportunity. I'm glad that there are mentoring programs to attract women into cybersecurity careers, and we should bring more awareness to others in our community about these mentoring opportunities and encourage local mentoring groups as well.

*It is widely known that cyber security is still a very male dominated industry, even though it is 2024. Why do you think there are so few women in cyber security?*

People still tend to think of cybersecurity as a career for men. Movies and shows often depict the characters who work in cybersecurity as men who work in a basement while wearing hoodies all day and night hacking various systems surrounded by numerous monitors. Women might not see themselves in those kinds of characters and wrongfully assume that they do not have a place in cybersecurity when that is not true at all! There's a misconception in the media that everyone in cybersecurity is introverted and a hacker. Cybersecurity professionals come from a wide variety of backgrounds and have different kinds of personalities. There are even cybersecurity jobs in technical sales which require you to talk to people all day. Not all jobs in cybersecurity require coding or scripting ability; there are some roles that are looking for that skillset (cybersecurity engineers, for example), but there are so many other roles that are looking for other skills like risk management, governance, or the ability to communicate technical cybersecurity concepts to non-technical audiences.

I'm glad there are more initiatives designed to encourage women to pursue tech and cybersecurity careers; it would be nice to have more movies and TV shows that depict real cybersecurity professionals to show how there is a place for everyone in cybersecurity.

*Who are your role models in cyber security?*

I have so many role models in cybersecurity that it is so difficult to list out just a few of them. But here are the first few role models that come to mind.

One of my role models in cybersecurity is Yolanda Reid; she was my Women in CyberSecurity (WiCyS) mentor and I learned so much from her. I've met with Yolanda for years now and have always learned so much from our conversations. She helped me when I was first starting out in the field and advised me on how to navigate the workplace as one of the only women. During the mentoring program, we talked about how to move up the career ladder, how to negotiate my salary and how to apply to jobs. One piece of advice she gave me was to negotiate and ask for what you want in an offer. It does not hurt to ask; if you don't ask, the answer is automatically a "no" anyway. So, it's better to ask for what you want.

Yolanda also inspired me to invest in my own skillset and pursue professional development programs. She encouraged me to apply for the doctoral program in cybersecurity analytics. I had come across the doctoral program in an email, but I was hesitant to apply; that evening, I decided to message Yolanda about it. She encouraged me to apply for the program and said I could do it. Her encouragement helped me gain more confidence in myself, and because of that encouragement, I ultimately decided to apply for the doctoral program. I have learned so much from my mentors throughout my career, and I highly encourage others in the field to get a mentor or multiple mentors especially when you are early in your career. There are many different outreach organizations that have mentoring programs; the organization that I used for finding my cybersecurity mentor was Women in CyberSecurity (WiCyS), but there are other organizations out there as well.

Jen Easterly, the director of the US Cybersecurity and Infrastructure Security Agency (CISA) is another one of my role models. I am so inspired by her journey. She is definitely an inspiration for a lot of women. I used to work at CISA, and Director Easterly was an inspiring leader. While I was at CISA, I really appreciated her initiatives. She created programs to ensure that employees had appropriate mental health resources available and held numerous town halls throughout the year that did not just update us on the status of the organization but were also interactive and provided useful employee resources.

One town hall conversation that will always stay with me is a presentation by a guest speaker who talked about appreciating the little breaks you get in between meetings. We tend to think that 5 minutes is a very short amount of time, and one cannot possibly accomplish anything in 5 minutes. However, this guest speaker said that we can use those moments to do something that helps us reset, relax, and spark some joy before heading into our next meeting. For example, you can take 5 minutes to do a few simple stretches at your desk, eat a snack, or just do nothing and close your eyes and relax.

I really appreciated how she openly discussed prioritizing mental health especially during the pandemic. She encouraged us to follow her leadership philosophy principles, which I admire. Some of her leadership principles that stand out are leading with empathy, fostering belonging, diversity and inclusion, and a commitment to lifelong learning. She repeatedly told the workforce how she was committed to ensure that CISA was an organization which had an environment in which people would feel psychologically safe, and I think that is so important. I admire her so much and try to apply some of her leadership principles to my own life.

*If you could go back in time to your first days in the industry, what would you do differently or tell yourself?*

I would tell myself that it is okay to be myself and display my true personality at work. I should not have to pretend to like the same things that my peers like or try to morph myself into a cloned version of my peers. I need to be true to myself.

When I first began my career, I felt slightly nervous because I was one of the few women on the team. During the early stages of my career, I thought I had to change the way I dressed and avoid wearing dresses to be taken seriously. Or that I had to hide my long hair to be "professional". But over time, I learned that I need to be true to myself. I should wear business appropriate clothes that make me feel comfortable and confident instead of trying to blend in and wear something that resembles what my male colleagues might wear.

I know a lot of people in computer science and in cybersecurity are introverted, but I've always enjoyed talking to people and I would say I am not an introvert at all. Instead of trying to force myself to be someone I am not, I am learning to embrace my own strengths and true personality so that I can have a successful and enjoyable career.

*If you could give women considering a career in cybersecurity one piece of advice, what would it be?*

Go for it. Follow your passion and don't let anyone bring you down.

*And finally, tell us a few fun things about yourself! Do you have an unusual hobby for example, or a fun fact about yourself that you can share?*

I love travelling and exploring the world. I love learning about different cultures and appreciating the marvels in other cities. So far, I've been to 12 countries. I would love to continue travelling and meet some new people along the way!

# Saja Aljulaud

**Job Title:** Sr Information Security Analyst

**Company/Organisation:** Mastercard

*Tell us a bit about your background, your career to date and what you currently do in cyber security.*

Born and raised in Saudi Arabia, I had my Bachelor of Science in Computer Science from Saudi. I found myself at a crossroads after graduation. I didn't know what job to apply to. unsure of where my career path would lead me. The job market seemed inaccessible, like a closed circle. And the opportunities I found didn't align with my goals.

I spent a year applying to all sorts of jobs, with no luck.. Feeling lost and uncertain of what's next, I remembered a class in security during my undergrads that had caught my interest. So I decided to pursue a Master's in Information Systems Security, got nothing to lose anyways. I got accepted at University of Houston, Texas. It was during those two years in Houston that I found my passion for cybersecurity, and I had a little bit of clarity of what kind of career I want to pursue.

After completing my master's degree, I went back to Saudi, and started my professional journey as an Access Management Analyst, where I learned a lot about creating roles, groups and everything related to Active Directory, I enjoyed it so much that I installed my own AD in my personal computer so I can play a little bit with it -my boss at that time didn't want me to mess with users accounts, "they're real people, Saja!" he used to say, so a small AD on my computer it is!-

I moved to Vulnerability Management, where I discovered the importance of both technical expertise and interpersonal skills. As a team lead in this function, I learned how to bridge the gap between technical knowledge and effective communication, persuading departments and stakeholders of the criticality of patching on time.

It was then I started thinking about professional certificates, I wanted to get CISSP, even though I didn't have enough experience to support it, I said why not, I can be andAssociate of Isc2 working towards the CISSP. I have the technical knowledge, and a little bit of management. Dealing with all the managers from different departments for the vulnerability management

gave me a little bit of understanding of the way they think, what's their priorities, it was part of the reason why I felt confident about passing my CISSP, all I have to do is think when reading the questions :" what would manager x do in this situation", it worked! And I passed the exam!

It was all fun, till I was offered to lead the Network Team. Wanting to expand my horizons further, I jumped!, I found a new set of challenges and thrills there. Troubleshooting network issues, whether caused by an attacker or routine updates, became a source of excitement for me. I've learned to embrace the unpredictability of incidents, even if it means jumping into action at 2 AM, I remember these calls fondly, but not planning to go back to it though .

Needing a little bit of work life balance, I was offered a great opportunity to work on Security Strategy. In London, I accepted and I'm still learning and enjoying it.

I'm a big believer in giving back to the community. I volunteer with the ISC2 London Chapter and serve as the Women in Cybersecurity UKI Community Lead, where I am dedicated to ensuring that women are not only hired but also have opportunities to advance in their careers in cybersecurity.

Currently, I continue to work in the field of cybersecurity, leveraging my diverse skill set and experiences to help women in cyber wherever it's needed. My journey thus far has taught me resilience, adaptability, and the importance of continuous learning in an ever-evolving landscape of cyber threats.

*How did you get into the field of cyber security?*

My journey wasn't straightforward at all. After finishing my Bachelor's in Computer Science back home in Saudi Arabia, I found myself in this weird situation. I was applying for every job I found in my way, but nothing seemed to work. It was frustrating, to say the least.

Being the first daughter and granddaughter to graduate in my family, there was a lot of pressure on me to figure things out. Getting a job. A good one. It was the only question anyone would ask when they see my face "Hey! Did you get a job yet?" "Have you applied to XYZ?". It wasn't fun at all. I had no clue where to start. I remember scrolling through job listings, sending my CV to random people claiming they're hiring for their companies, feeling more and more lost with each rejection or irrelevant job offer.

It hit me one day that I liked cyber security since my undergrad, why not get a master in security, which I eventually did. I started applying, got accepted in University of Houston, and the rest is history!

I enjoyed my masters so much, I soaked up everything I could about cybersecurity! When I returned to Saudi Arabia after my studies, I was on a mission. I started applying for cybersecurity roles. And you know what? I finally got my foot in the door as an Access Management Analyst, wasn't bad at all :)

Looking back, I realize that my journey into cybersecurity wasn't easy, it took some time to figure things out, but it was mine. And it's led me to a career that I'm genuinely passionate about. Every day brings new challenges and opportunities for growth, and I'm really grateful for it.

*What are the main challenges you've encountered as a woman in cyber security, and how did you overcome them?*

There are many challenges that I've faced since I started my journey, some of them were actually fun.. Others were unbearable.

My first one was being the first and only female in my team. It posed its own set of challenges. I often found myself in situations where I had to educate my colleagues on appropriate behavior and language in the workplace (they were cool about it, they even started asking me if it's okay to say this or that, when is it mansplaining and when is it not?). It was a delicate balance of advocating for myself while also fostering a respectful and inclusive environment for everyone on the team. I enjoyed this one, wasn't bad at all

Another challenge I faced was the lack of representation of women in leadership roles within the cybersecurity industry. It was depressing, knowing that you have a small chance to be in a high level/management role.. However, it is not the same now. I'm so excited and happy that it is changing and I can see it across multiple organizations.

*What are the things you've learned being a woman in the cyber security industry?*

I've learned a lot being women working in the industry, I've learned to be resilient in the face of adversity. Whether it's overcoming gender bias, or navigating challenging situations,

I've learned the importance of mentorship and support networks in navigating the challenges of being a woman in cybersecurity. Or any challenge that faces me in general. Seeking guidance from mentors, connecting with other professionals in the industry, and offering support to others have been a game changer in my professional development and personal growth

Women in the cybersecurity industry are incredibly welcoming. Don't be afraid to reach out and ask questions. Get a mentor who can offer guidance and support as you navigate your career. And remember, don't be afraid of rejection. Trust me, it's not the end of the world, its part of life.

*What advice would you give to women who would like to join the cyber security industry?*

If I could give women considering a career in cybersecurity one piece of advice, it would be this: Believe in yourself and don't be afraid of this field, it's just a job just like anything else. .

Entering a male-dominated field like cybersecurity can feel daunting and a little bit scary, but it's important to recognize your abilities, talent and trust in yourself. Don't let yourself hold you back from pursuing a career that excites and challenges you whether it's in cyber or anything else in life. .

Be proud of your unique perspective and the diverse skills you bring to the table. You might not know it, but your contributions are always invaluable to the community.

Seek out mentorship and support networks to help navigate the challenges you may face along the way. You're not alone, and whatever issue you're facing I can guarantee that there are at least 10 people out there facing the same one, don't take it all on yourself.

Surround yourself with allies who uplift and empower you, and don't hesitate to advocate for yourself and others.

Remember, you have the power to shape the future of cybersecurity and make a meaningful impact on the community - no pressure though-. So, never underestimate the value of your presence and contributions in the field.

You belong here, and the cybersecurity industry is better with you in it.

*What role does diversity play in cyber security?*

Diversity in the workplace, whether in Cyber or any industry, celebrates the richness of varied perspectives, experiences, and problem-solving approaches, bridging gaps present in homogeneous groups. It's a catalyst for creativity, innovation, and heightened cultural awareness. By embracing diverse viewpoints, we not only attract top talent from underrepresented communities but also confront biases head-on. This inclusive environment nurtures out-of-the-box thinking and cultivates cutting-edge security technologies and strategies. Ultimately, it's about empowering individuals from all backgrounds to contribute their unique strengths, fostering resilience and effectiveness in our security practices.

*It is widely known that cyber security is still a very male dominated industry, even though it is 2024. Why do you think there are so few women in cyber security?*

Thats a complex issue with several contributing factors, historically our field has always been male-dominated. This imbalance has persisted over time and has influenced the composition of the cybersecurity workforce.

There are also stereotypes and biases, gender stereotypes and biases can prevent women from pursuing careers in cybersecurity.

Cultural norms may also steer women away from technical fields, leading to fewer female candidates entering the cybersecurity workforce. Even though we also have a nontechnical side of cyber security

One of the important factors is workplace Culture and Environment. A lack of diversity and inclusion in cybersecurity organizations can create unwelcoming environments for women.

Addressing the underrepresentation of women in cybersecurity requires a lot of work, I'm so happy and privileged to be part of Women in Cybersecurity UKI. the work they do in the organization is amazing for uplifting women in cyber. Helping in the recruitment and retention of women in UKI .I know we are not going to solve the issue, but at least we are trying to bbe part of the solutions

*Who are your role models in cyber security?*

Zinet Kemal is forever my role model. She started her security career around 2020 but my god how she worked so hard on herself and her personal brand that she's a well known security practitioner now! She's also a book author, she writes children books about cybersecurity, and how to be safe online. Her books are about uplifting and empowering girls to be proud of themselves and identities, create awareness for diversity and inclusion, and she won so many awards as an author, I'm so inspired by her journey

*If you could go back in time to your first days in the industry, what would you do differently or tell yourself?*

A lot! I've learned a lot that I wish I could tell my younger-self of any young women trying to pursue a corporate career, but the important ones are as follow:

**Trust Yourself more:** I would remind myself to have confidence in my skills and knowledge. It's easy to doubt yourself when entering a new field, especially one as technical and fast-paced as cybersecurity.

**Seek mentorship:** seeking mentorship early in your career is absolutely crucial—I can't emphasize enough how important it is. If I could go back, I would encourage myself to seek out mentors and role models in the industry right from the beginning. It would have saved me a lot of time and effort. Currently, I have two mentors who have been invaluable in my professional development journey, and I also serve as a mentor myself. I really can't stress enough how much of a game-changer mentorship has been for me. The challenge lies in picking mentors who are the right fit for you and your needs, but once you find them, the benefits are immeasurable.

**Don't Be Afraid to Ask Questions:** I would always remind myself that it's okay to ask questions and seek clarification when faced with uncertainty. Asking questions is not a sign of weakness but rather a demonstration of curiosity and a desire to learn and grow, and trust me, if the question crossed your mind, I'm sure others have the same uncertainty too, so don't feel like it a sign of weakness at all.

**Prioritize Work-Life Balance:** It's super easy to get caught up in the demands of a new job or industry, but taking time for self-care and personal interests is essential for long-term success and fulfillment.

And finally, never forget the importance of recognizing and celebrating my achievements. it's essential to advocate for yourself and ensure that your accomplishments are acknowledged.Don't be afraid to speak up about your successes and the impact you've made. Whether it's implementing a new security measure that significantly reduces vulnerabilities, leading a successful incident response effort, or earning certifications to enhance your skills, your achievements deserve recognition!!

Remember, "it's not bragging if it's based on facts". So, be proud of what you've accomplished, and don't hesitate to showcase your achievements.

*And finally, tell us a few fun things about yourself! Do you have an unusual hobby for example, or a fun fact about yourself that you can share?*

Of course! Here are a few fun things about me:

**Baking Enthusiast:** In my free time, I love to experiment with new baking recipes. There's something incredibly therapeutic about mixing ingredients together and creating delicious treats from scratch.

**Lifelong Learner:** I have a passion for learning and exploring new skills. Whether it's diving into a new language, or delving into a new hobby, I'm always eager to expand my knowledge and challenge myself.

**Volunteer Work:** Giving back to my community is important to me, and I'm actively involved in volunteer work. Whether it's supporting local charities, mentoring aspiring cybersecurity professionals, or participating in community events, I find fulfillment in making a positive impact in the lives of others.

These are just a few fun things about me! I believe in living life to the fullest, embracing new experiences, and finding joy in the little moments.

# Gabrielle Botbol

**Job Title:** Offensive Security Consultant

**Company/Organisation:** Desjardins and CSbyGB

*Tell us a bit about your background, your career to date and what you currently do in cyber security.*

In high school, I pursued arts and literature to become an actress. However, my passion for programming flourished at home, particularly in creating theater-related websites. Despite this interest, I hesitated to pursue studies in computer science due to the expectations of my parents and school teachers, who envisioned me in the field of literature. Consequently, I pursued acting and worked as a hotel receptionist.

Yet, my enthusiasm for programming continued to grow, and fifteen years ago, during a working holiday visa in Canada, I seized the opportunity to delve into IT. Upon returning to France, I decided to earn a bachelor's degree in computer science.

A few years later, I trained myself to become a pentester.

Now, I have been thriving in this role for approximately five years.

My work consists of testing systems to check if they have vulnerabilities.

I enjoy it because every day is different, and I am constantly learning new things because technologies evolve fast.

It's a rewarding job because it aligns with my values, and every day I work, I humbly contribute to enhancing security within my company and, by extension, for the citizens.

*How did you get into the field of cyber security?*

While working as a developer in a large company, I became increasingly concerned about the security of the applications I was delivering.

This led me to embark on a journey to become a pentester. Because of the lack of fitting training programs or their prohibitive costs, I resolved to create my own self-taught program. Drawing inspiration from the concept of

"Apprenance," by Philippe Carré, which briefly says that learning can take many different forms and be achieved in many different situations.

This is how I structured my program into six key steps:

1. E-learning: Delving into cybersecurity fundamentals.

2. Conferences: Engaging with professionals, networking, and exploring diverse cybersecurity topics.

3. Capture The Flag (CTF): Practicing cybersecurity skills interactively and enjoyably.

4. Internships: Gaining firsthand industry experience.

5. Volunteering: Connecting with like-minded individuals and expanding professional networks.

6. Learning expeditions: Exploring academic research in cybersecurity through visits to institutions such as Polytechnic of Lviv in Ukraine, NATO Europol, and Leiden University in the Netherlands.

I meticulously documented my journey in a blog.

During this period, I also started to look for job opportunities. I did not find many in France, so I applied to international job fairs, and that is how I found my first position as a pentester in Canada.

*What are the main challenges you've encountered as a woman in cyber security, and how did you overcome them?*

My main challenges as a woman in cybersecurity revolve around biases. Working with individuals with preconceived notions about women in the tech industry is challenging.

Some biases persist, such as the belief that women are not technical.

Therefore, I've had to constantly justify and fight twice as hard, even today, to be taken seriously in my practice.

Additionally, I've observed that it's not always well-received to have developed complementary skills alongside technical expertise, such as communication. Some view this as a threat to the exclusivity of the technical cybersecurity community, fearing the popularization of complex techniques and potential risks to their closed and elitist circle.

To overcome these challenges, I've remained steadfast in my dedication to my work, consistently demonstrating my technical proficiency and effectively communicating the value of diverse skill sets in cybersecurity.

I've also sought out supportive networks and allies within the industry to advocate for equal recognition and opportunities.

*What are the things you've learned being a woman in the cyber security industry?*

One positive aspect I've noticed is the increasing number of initiatives and events aimed at giving voice to women in the cybersecurity industry.

On the flip side, a negative aspect is that we are often pigeonholed into discussing topics solely related to the role of women rather than our respective specialties.

Despite the lack of expectation for our presence, we can sometimes be heard when we assert ourselves and contribute to discussions with our arguments. It's our responsibility to participate, even though it can be challenging at times because technology cannot be created and directed solely by a segment of the population; after all, it's humanity as a whole that utilizes these technologies.

*What advice would you give to women who would like to join the cyber security industry?*

If you face rejection from employers, it's essential not to lose hope.

Instead, focus on emphasizing your transferable skills, setting clear goals and deadlines for yourself, and actively seeking assistance and support from the cybersecurity community.

It's crucial to remember that developing a hacker mindset takes time and dedication.

Don't be discouraged by initial setbacks; with perseverance, you can enhance your skills and adapt to the challenges of the field.

Additionally, consider that transitioning to a completely different career path can present valuable learning and personal growth opportunities. Embrace the chance to expand your knowledge and capabilities in cybersecurity, leveraging your existing skills while remaining open to new experiences.

*What role does diversity play in cyber security?*

Diversity plays a pivotal role in cybersecurity, as it fosters an inclusive, respectful, and equitable working environment that benefits both individuals and the company as a whole.

Recognizing the importance of allyship goes beyond addressing gender disparities; it becomes an economic imperative for the company's success.

Throughout history, diverse perspectives and experiences have fueled innovation worldwide.

This underscores the significance of collaboration and embracing varied viewpoints in driving change and progress within companies and societies.

By extending a universal invitation to all individuals to contribute to the solution, we fortify our defense mechanisms and take a significant stride toward achieving Cyberpeace.

*It is widely known that cyber security is still a very male dominated industry, even though it is 2024. Why do you think there are so few women in cyber security?*

Several factors contribute to this disparity.

Firstly, there is a pervasive issue of unconscious biases that affect hiring and promotion practices within companies. Training programs for business leaders and executives to address and overcome these biases are crucial in creating a more inclusive workplace environment.

Secondly, retaining talented women in cybersecurity remains a considerable challenge that demands focused attention. This challenge is exacerbated by systemic barriers, including wage disparities, impediments to career progression, and ingrained unconscious biases prevalent within the industry.

Moreover, the lack of support systems and networking

opportunities further compounds the issue. Women often find themselves isolated or without the necessary support mechanisms critical for professional growth and development within cybersecurity, prompting them to seek alternative career paths.

Furthermore, the pervasive issues of sexism and workplace harassment persist within the cybersecurity field, contributing to a hostile work environment for many women. These systemic challenges undermine efforts to retain female talent, leading to a significant departure of women who feel marginalized or undervalued.

Finally, amplifying the profiles of individuals from underrepresented communities, including women, within the industry is essential. Increasing visibility and representation through initiatives such as spotlighting employees' profiles on social networks can inspire and motivate aspiring professionals. Seeing women in leadership positions within cybersecurity can empower other women to pursue careers in this field.

Addressing systemic biases and actively promoting diversity and inclusion within the cybersecurity industry is essential to creating a more equitable and representative workforce.

*Who are your role models in cyber security?*

Alissa Knight, Tanya Janca

*If you could go back in time to your first days in the industry, what would you do differently or tell yourself?*

I would tell myself that I have no reason to feel ashamed and that I belong here just as much as anyone else. Additionally, I would remind myself that thanks to my perseverance, I will achieve goals in the future that I hadn't even imagined.

I would also advise myself not to listen to negative voices.

My technical prowess helps me in my daily practice, but my soft skills make me a more humane individual in this field and allow me to provide a better job.

*If you could give women considering a career in cybersecurity one piece of advice, what would it be?*

Make a list of activities you enjoy doing. Look at job postings and university curricula to gain insight into the roles that best suit your interests in the field. Don't hesitate to seek advice from experts in the field to understand what they enjoy about their jobs. This will help you identify the role that aligns best with your passions and will make you excited to get out of bed every morning.

*And finally, tell us a few fun things about yourself! Do you have an unusual hobby for example, or a fun fact about yourself that you can share?*

I love fashion, so I felt somewhat limited when I heard hackers only wore hoodies.

But on a more serious note, I believe that dressing in a way that reflects our personal style allows us, as cybersecurity professionals, to showcase our diversity.

In a way, it brings us closer to others because, as you may have noticed, the stereotypical image of a hacker in a black hoodie and mask can be pretty intimidating.

# Emily Bridge

**Job Title:** Cyber Incident Response Consultant

**Company/Organisation:** Deloitte

*Tell us a bit about your background, your career to date and what you currently do in cyber security.*

I have only just started my career as of August 2023, after completing my degree at my local college. At University I studied Digital Leadership, which covered modules such as cybersecurity, web development and graphics and I also completed my CIM Level 6 in Digital Marketing and CMI Certificate in Business and Leadership. Since starting work, I have got to work on major incidents, which I love so far as every day I get to learn from the experts and contribute to real-life projects. I am also currently revising for my Blue Team Level 1 exam, so when I am not at work, I am hitting the books, so I am certainly kept busy!

*How did you get into the field of cyber security?*

I knew from a young age that I always wanted to go into something Technology related and a cyber security crash course happened to take place at my Secondary school so I went along to expand my knowledge. That is where I fell in love with Cyber Security as there are so many streams you can take, such as offensive and defensive security, cloud security, etc. My dad happens to work in offensive security and I would read his books, which is where my passion came from. As well as getting hands-on in offensive security, I also enjoy the more defensive side as to learn to break into something, you need to know how it is made! In the future, I hope to become Purple Team, so I can put my out-of-work learning into my career!

*What are the main challenges you've encountered as a woman in cyber security, and how did you overcome them?*

One of the biggest challenges I have found is walking into a project team and it being all males. This I found was especially visible in Uni, as I was one of 2 girls in a class of 10! It was quite funny in group work as they would automatically designate you to be the 'artist' or more business management, so when I talk about cyber topics they look at me in confusion, as they stereotype that women don't know anything about cyber. Another thing which I luckily haven't experienced yet but have been warned happens to all cyber security professionals is Imposter Syndrome. From speaking with colleagues, they have warned me that the impact can be quite detrimental, however the biggest piece of advice I have been told is that your career is a journey, celebrate the small wins and focus on yourself. The cyber industry can be very chaotic, so you shouldn't feel guilty about having some 'me' time or saying no. You should never suffer alone in silence, speak up as if you are struggling, nobody will know unless you say!

*What are the things you've learned being a woman in the cyber security industry?*

It is a very male-dominated industry, however, each day you are seeing more women. I have learnt to be proud of being a Woman in Cyber. It is also a very motivating community, as within the Network we share opportunities to help each other. The Women in Cyber is almost like a family as we support each other and I have loved being able to connect with others online and learn from them, especially as we all come from different backgrounds and have different experiences!

*What advice would you give to women who would like to join the cyber security industry?*

As I have just begun my cyber career, I reflect on it often. My biggest piece of advice is to go for it! You can dream of being the next leading woman in cyber all you want, but to achieve this dream you need to work hard and it does pay off! As the saying goes, "work hard and play hard". Be curious and ask loads of questions, your biggest way to grow is to use those around you. Take any opportunity you have and enjoy every moment. Make sure to take risks too, you can stay in your comfort zone all you want, but to follow your dreams, you need to do things you never thought of doing.

Make your dreams a reality, you have got this!

*What role does diversity play in cyber security?*

I think diversity plays a huge role as you can learn so much from different people. Cyber isn't a one-fit role, therefore be sure to ask questions to those around you and learn from the best. The biggest thing about cyber is that it is in your heart, so share your passion with those around you. What I love about the diversity of cyber is that there are so many ages, I have worked with those similar age to me and those a lot older. Age is becoming more of a contribution to the diversity within cyber as at the beginning, the workforce entered this 'new' industry, but now with the rise of the Digital Age, more 'Gen Z' are entering as cyber is becoming more 'trendy'.

*It is widely known that cyber security is still a very male dominated industry, even though it is 2024. Why do you think there are so few women in cyber security?*

As Cyber is fairly new and emerging, I think that is the main contribution to the lack of women. Additionally, I think the negative stereotypes held also play a part. Therefore these women in cyber networks are so empowering as it shows that anyone can do a job and flourish, no matter their age, gender, sexual orientation, race, etc. One of the main reasons I believe we lack women in cyber is because there is not much representation. For example, on the news, most cyber correspondents are males, which creates the idea that women are not meant for the industry. Another reason I believe is stereotypes. If you search up 'cyber' most the images are males, in hoodies sat next to a screen in a dark room; we need more female representation as I believe it will encourage and inspire more women to take up this career field.

*Who are your role models in cyber security?*

One of my biggest role models is Cyber Sec Meg as following her Twitter account, I find her tweets so relatable. Another person I look up to is FreakyClown (FC) as I have been lucky enough to attend his talks and enjoyed his stories, additionally, his wife, Dr Jessica Barker, is constantly active online and sharing such amazing insights into her experience and how she came to be where she is now. Finally, 2 people I have been lucky to work with are Danni Brooke and Ben Owen from Hunted UK. They have been so supportive in my career as I regularly share my journey so far with them and I enjoyed getting time with them to chat about cyber and their time on Hunted, such as their experiences in the HQ and how they managed to find people.

This isn't a 'cyber-influencer' as such but without sounding cheesy, the biggest role model to me is my Dad. He was the one who introduced me to Cyber and without his support throughout my studies, I do not think I would be where I am today.

*If you could go back in time to your first days in the industry, what would you do differently or tell yourself?*

One of the biggest mistakes I made at work was walking in and being nervous that I will be 'a failure'. This wasn't the case. What I would do differently is certainly make more time to meet up with my team and to learn from their experiences. I also remember feeling a bit of an odd one out in my predominantly male lecture, so I wish I just 'owned it'. I felt ashamed to be the only woman in my classes, so I should've been proud that I was changing this.

*If you could give women considering a career in cybersecurity one piece of advice, what would it be?*

Use those around you! You can Google all the answers you want, but one of the best ways to flourish is to collaborate with others and hear their experiences! I found hearing so many different experiences of people made me realise my worth as I came to realise that I do belong and there are no criteria for being in the cyber industry, the only criteria in reality is having a passion and working for it!

*And finally, tell us a few fun things about yourself! Do you have an unusual hobby for example, or a fun fact about yourself that you can share?*

1. I nearly got to represent my area at the 2019 Code Like a Girl Hackathon in London, however, due to Covid, that didn't happen.

2. In my spare time, I love content creation and I regularly make content about my career in Cyber and the perspective of a 'Grad' entering the industry. I share my experiences and insights into my days, to break the stigma that cyber is sitting in a dark room with a hoodie on at a computer, as no way is that true! Every day is so different!

3. In my spare time, I love to volunteer and make a difference. I have been fortunate to win many awards for it and I find that giving back is so rewarding and I feel a sense of pride at events. Some of the feedback I receive sticks with me and knowing I make a difference to at least 1 person fills me with joy.

# Rebecca Caldwell

**Job Title:** Content Specialist and Research

**Company/Organisation:** Phriendly Phishing

*Tell us a bit about your background, your career to date and what you currently do in cyber security.*

I have had a varied career, I like variety. I started out in film and television as an actor and presenter working in hospitality to make ends meet, as many do in that industry! I eventually took a marketing job at a data communications engineering firm where I was given the opportunity to learn how to manage the website and online presence – this lead me into SEO when it was in it's infancy as an industry and it's where I sat for well over 8 years before moving into project management and leadership. I kept dabbling in TV in between all this to stay creative, and I bring little bit of each of those worlds with me into my role today. At Phriendly Phishing I write content for customers, marketing and promotions and I am also empowered to research or assist other teams including course creation, sales enablement and website content.

*How did you get into the field of cyber security?*

I live in Melbourne, Australia and we were in hard lock-down for almost two years, the longest stretch was around 260 days straight of being confined to the home for 23 hours a day. I quickly got sick of my routine and took the chance and left my full time job and went to university and did a one year course in Cyber to switch things up. It was difficult learning from home but I did it!

*What are the main challenges you've encountered as a woman in cyber security, and how did you overcome them?*

To be honest, my own limiting thoughts. I know I'm a capable person, but entering a new industry at my age was daunting and I began by looking for IT help desk jobs. After a stern talking to from a good career coach, I started applying for more mature roles, and I was lucky enough to find one that combined my new fledgling knowledge with my past experience.

*What are the things you've learned being a woman in the cyber security industry?*

That in many ways, it's no different to any other industry – there will always be a boys club culture in some organisations and especially specific roles and you just have to be ready to speak up and take your space. From a fulfillment point of view – for people like me who thrive on learning, it's a fantastic industry as there is NEVER a day when you'll know everything. There are so many pathways and they are all interesting so it's like being a kid in a candy store for the cyber polymath.

*What advice would you give to women who would like to join the cyber security industry?*

You can do it at any age, you just need the curiosity and of course time to learn. If you don't fit into the technical side, take a look at your existing skills and see where they fit. There's definitely space for you.

*What role does diversity play in cyber security?*

A very important one. Since cyber issues are rarely just one issue in isolation, a wide range of skill sets and ways of thinking are needed to solve them. For example, I used to do email marketing in my early career and I encountered almost every way possible to spoof an email and 'from' address – but to the uninitiated, I was just a girl from an advertising agency wanting to have a say into how phishing works and how to spot it to the team. Listening to people when they know more than you, even when it's ultra niche, is diversity at play.

*It is widely known that cyber security is still a very male dominated industry, even though it is 2024. Why do you think there are so few women in cyber security?*

Many women might think it's a long term, highly technical job that is fairly thankless. A lot of women I talk to don't see the emotional payoff in jobs like this, but it is there in that you are either saving the day for a customer, or learning a new way of doing something and teaching others. Some parts can be hard, like any job, but choose your stream wisely and it's really fulfilling. Also remember women are the pioneers of cyber security and computer science, so embrace that you belong there.

*Who are your role models in cyber security?*

There are so many female founders in Cyber Security and AI that I admire, I don't want to leave anyone out but I'm following many on linkedin. From a personal perspective, the amazing female leadership team at Phriendly Phishing are definitely a team to be reckoned with and have shown me that empathy does exist in the tech space.

*If you could go back in time to your first days in the industry, what would you do differently or tell yourself?*

I still consider myself emerging in this industry so I'd be interested in some of the other answers here! I suppose the one thing I would have done differently would have been to start sooner.

*If you could give women considering a career in cybersecurity one piece of advice, what would it be?*

It's never too late, and you DO already have some of the skills you need to succeed.

*And finally, tell us a few fun things about yourself! Do you have an unusual hobby for example, or a fun fact about yourself that you can share?*

I love a varied existence, it's what attracted me to cyber –
Outside of work, I love to collect art from emerging artists,
I participate in local theatre and I make my own pickles.

# Jan Carroll

**Job Title:** Cybersecurity Educator/Founder

**Company/Organisation:** Fortify Institute

*Tell us a bit about your background, your career to date and what you currently do in cyber security.*

I've always worked in technology. When I left school in the early 90s, I worked as an apprentice electrician and when I got fed up with working on the sites, I went to college to study electronics while working nights as a technician in a factory. A few years later, I was working in a college in computer services when I had my third child. I took a break for a couple of years to be at home and when I returned to working I needed a job that was flexible. This in when I moved in to teaching. I took on a role as an

IT trainer in a further education centre. It didn't take me
long to realise that even though I had the tech skills, I
didn't have the teaching skills and I returned to college
part-time to complete a teacher training and eventually a
MEd in Adult & Community Education.

At that time I was teaching people who all had varying barriers and challenges when it came to education.
I worked with Traveller women, teens who didn't attend
mainstream education, recent immigrants and adults taking advantage of second-chance education. It was a wonderful learning environment and I saw the benefits to all
by making education and learning accessible and flexible
for the learner. When I set up Fortify Institute, making
the learning accessible for all was a key goal. How I got
to the point of setting up a cyber training company was
one day, with the adult learners, we were chatting about
what we would do if we had our time again. I was asked
what I would do. I said, without hesitation, cybersecurity.
By the end of that week, I had enrolled in a MSc in Applied Cybersecurity part-time course, and graduated with
a first, two years later. After I graduated, I sought work in
the booming cybersecurity sector in Ireland. It was around
the time GDPR was introduced so there were lots of opportunities.

Over the next few years I was lucky to work in some of
the best cyber companies in Ireland. Then covid hit and
brought lockdown. Like many, I took this time to take
stock and I realised that I missed teaching. I was long
enough in cybersecurity to know that there was a huge
skills gap and a lack of diversity issue. I hadn't considered
starting my own business before but there's a long tradi-
tion of women entrepreneurs in my family, so I took the
leap. I founded Fortify Institute in 2022 and offer flexible

cybersecurity, ethical hacking and cloud security training to professionals. I also work with other training providers, such as UCD Professional Academy and Chevron College/University of Sunderland to create and deliver their cyber programmes. Fortify Institute is the first EC-Council accredited training centre in the Republic of Ireland, and we're authorised training centre for the Cloud Security Alliance and CompTIA offering their range of courses.

One benefit of working for myself is I can choose to dedicate time to volunteering, community endeavours and lifelong learning. I'm on an ENISA ad-hoc working group. I am on the Cyber Ireland

Business Growth Committee. I'm a member of WiCyS and other women in business and women in tech communities. I'm part of the support team for Ireland's entry to the European Cybersecurity Challenge CTF. I was previously on the Ireland Cyber Awareness Task Force which created resources for frontline workers to support victims of tech facilitated abuse.

I have recently embarked on a professional doctorate to research a topic which will have a huge benefit to the cybersecurity community and national security of Ireland.

*How did you get into the field of cyber security?*

Think I covered that above. Here are some profiles[1][2]

*What are the main challenges you've encountered as a woman in cyber security, and how did you overcome them?*

---

[1] https://insights.pecb.com/my-success-story-jan-carroll/
[2] https://www.innovationacademy.ie/stories/unlock-your-ambition-think-big-and-find-the-enterprise-in-you/

Work life balance. My husband and I have 4 children, they're big now but it was tough when they were small. When I started working in cybersecurity, it was the first time, since having all 4 children that I was working full-time. I overcame this by working from home as much as possible. Since starting Fortify Institute, I work from home all the time. Most of our programmes are delivered live, on-line. I have plans to deliver an in-person course this year and look forward to it. I love attending conferences and volunteer at events for the social aspect as much as for the networking.

I also suffer from imposter syndrome at times. As soon as I overcome that, I'll let you know.

*What are the things you've learned being a woman in the cyber security industry?*

When I worked as an electrician, I loved the work, but I never fit in. From the very basics of sites not having women's toilets to blatant sexism and sexist abuse. I was sad to leave but I wouldn't put up with it.

It is very different in cybersecurity. I know times have moved on, but I always felt I fit in. Everyone in the industry knows there should be more women and more diversity in general and are working towards improvement. There's room for everyone in the cyber security industry.

Don't get me wrong, there is still room for huge improvement, and I take solace in many of the women in cyber communities which champion the positive changes. This isn't an issues for only women to fix. We all benefit from increased diversity.

*What advice would you give to women who would like to*

*join the cyber security industry?*

Don't hesitate. Go for it. There are so many different roles that if you don't like one, you can switch to another.

Don't be too hard on yourself. Everyone is winging it.

You don't have to hit all the job spec requirements 100

Read Invisible Women by Caroline Criado Perez and get the men in your life to read it too.

*What role does diversity play in cyber security?*

Diversity improves security. We don't all think in the same way so having a diverse team enhances our abilities. A mix of cultures, neurodiversity, sexes etc will make for better defences and enhances security design.

*It is widely known that cyber security is still a very male dominated industry, even though it is 2024. Why do you think there are so few women in cyber security?*

We're looking at it from the inside out. Those of us who are in the industry think that everyone knows about the opportunities and they are choosing not to join this fantastic industry. The industry needs to be marketed to girls, young women and returners so they know that these roles exist.

There is still a lot of bias in job descriptions and the interview process. This needs to be urgently tackled.

We need to see it to be it. The more women we see on panels, the better. I've mixed feelings about this as we need to see women talking about their expertise, like the men are. However, often we see the women on panel discussing the challenges of being a women in tech.

*Who are your role models in cyber security?*

Jenny Radcliff, Wendy Nather, Valerie Lyons, Jennifer Cox.

*If you could go back in time to your first days in the industry, what would you do differently or tell yourself?*

I'm late to the industry, I was in my 40s when I made the jump. I'd encourage many to do the same at that stage. It addresses the skills gap and also offers opportunities to returners or those moving from other careers.

While I've no regrets, I'd probably have spent more time on selecting my first role. I took the first role I was offered as I was delighted to get it and terrified I wouldn't get another one.

*If you could give women considering a career in cybersecurity one piece of advice, what would it be?*

Do the tech stuff, especially early in your career. Get involved in the community, the CTFs, the OWASP Chapter meeting, the BSides Committees, the Women in Cyber groups.

*And finally, tell us a few fun things about yourself! Do you have an unusual hobby for example, or a fun fact about yourself that you can share?*

I'm a nerd and love learning. I have 11 degrees and embarking on a professional doctorate. I got into running when I was 40, I'm 50 this year and training for my 5th and final marathon. I play Gaelic football with a 'Mothers and

Others' team which is for women over 25 who just want to play for fun.

Taking a trip to Bletchley Park with my family this year.

# Dr Andrea Cullen

**Job Title:** Co-Founder

**Company/Organisation:** CAPSLOCK Education Ltd.

*Tell us a bit about your background, your career to date and what you currently do in cyber security.*

I have always worked in technology. I started working as a coder and later systems analyst. I then had a career break. After this I went to university as a mature student and did a BSc in Computer Science followed by a PhD in Operations Management. This was an ideal background for moving into cyber security. I started as an academic in

2003 and developed and launched one of the first MSc's in Cyber in the UK. It wasn't called cyber (the term didn't really exist) bit instead it was called Internet Computer and Systems Security. I worked in a university for 16 years at the same time as running a consultancy business.

After this time I worked at KPMG for a couple of year leading on internal cyber culture change amongst other projects. I started CAPSLOCK alongside my fellow co-founder Lorna Armitage, incorporated in 2019 and going live in early 2021. CAPSLOCK is a career changing boot-camp that offers those without a cyber background the opportunity to enter the sector. The whole ethos is about removing barriers to life changing education. As a startup I wear many hats both running the business and in the virtual classroom.

*How did you get into the field of cyber security?*

It was almost by accident, like most people at that time. Having a background in both technology and operations it was ideal experience and also joining an academic department at a time when security was just beginning to emerge. As an emerging topic, it was exciting to be able to research and develop something so cutting edge.

*What are the main challenges you've encountered as a woman in cyber security, and how did you overcome them?*

Being talked over and ignored can be a problem. The expectation is that if there is a man in the room, then they must be the expert.

I feel you have to both pick your battles and stand your ground in equal measures. I am a firm believer in role models. I look to these for inspiration and see that I am a role model to others. Speaking out and being visible are so important. Perhaps the wort behaviour is being constantly questioned and challenged and feeling like you have to authenticate yourself.

Overcoming these challenges can take some time but the first step is to speak out, be visible and find a supportive community (which cyber has many).

*What are the things you've learned being a woman in the cyber security industry?*

You need to be twice as good as a man for the half the rewards at time :D. I've learned that cyber can be enormously supportive - but it lacks diversity in many ways. Being a women I find I understand what being a minority in this sector means and it teaches you to be empathetic and supportive of others. It also spurs me on to do something practical about it. It has taught me that encouraging women into the sector is the responsibility of all of us.

*What advice would you give to women who would like to join the cyber security industry?*

Come in - it's amazing! Find your role models and mentors, and your community. Stand your ground and realise just how much you bring. Cyber needs diversity to reflect the society it is designed to protect. Get a plan and get support at each stage - there is plenty of people who are keen to offer this support and advice.

*What role does diversity play in cyber security?*

Diversity is so important as it brings diversity of thought and therefore better solutions. It's important to help cyber represent society in the broadest sense and this makes sure that we are all part of a solution rather than bolted on or an afterthought.

*It is widely known that cyber security is still a very male dominated industry, even though it is 2024. Why do you think there are so few women in cyber security?*

It think this is mostly the case that we keep doing the same things and expecting a different outcome. Cyber is perceived s a techy boys club, too difficult, not accessible and not interesting. It is also full of smoke and mirrors. The biggest change for me comes with a change in messaging and demystifying the sector. Secondly, we need to continue with role models - of all ages and at all stages of their careers.

*Who are your role models in cyber security?*

I have loads of role models for all aspects of a career in cyber from the knowledge, passion, hard work and commitment. My wife Lorna is the best cyber role model - she is passionate about breaking down barriers to entry into the sector and goes all out to make it happen.

*If you could go back in time to your first days in the industry, what would you do differently or tell yourself?*

Quite simply I'd be more confident and have much more self-belief.

*If you could give women considering a career in cybersecurity one piece of advice, what would it be?*

Don't say that you can't do something without adding "yet". Have faith in yourself as you bring something unique and important to the sector - having confidence takes you most of the way so make sure you devote time to developing yours.

*And finally, tell us a few fun things about yourself! Do you have an unusual hobby for example, or a fun fact about yourself that you can share?*

I can touch my nose with my tongue.

# Eleanor Dallaway

**Job Title:** Co-Founder and Editor

**Company/Organisation:** Assured (Co-Founder)/Assured Intelligence (Editor)

*Tell us a bit about your background, your career to date and what you currently do in cyber security.*

I entered the world of cyber journalism in 2006 as Assistant Editor for *Infosecurity* Magazine. Within 18 months, I was promoted to Editor, and later, publisher. During my time at *Infosecurity*, I advised the Conservative Government on their information security policies, won a few journalism awards, launched the Women in Cybersecurity network and event series, and turned a print-only publication into a digital and print product with eight million

57

readers a year by the time I left.

In 2022, I left *Infosecurity* to co-found a cyber insurance company, Assured, which is the only brokerage in the UK that focuses solely on cyber. I also launched *Assured Intelligence*, an editorially independent cybersecurity content platform and network for senior execs.

*How did you get into the field of cyber security?*

It's the clichéd answer: by accident. I was looking for a job in journalism after I graduated. Living in Oxford, I applied for reporter roles in Elsevier's B2B department and was offered the first job I interviewed for: Assistant Editor of *Infosecurity*. They kindly held the role for me while I backpacked around Europe for the summer. I saw it as a stepping stone into writing for more glamorous sectors (I had aspirations of *Grazia*, *Vogue* and *Elle*), but I fell in love with the sector and the rest, as they say, is history!

*What are the main challenges you've encountered as a woman in cyber security, and how did you overcome them?*

I can honestly say I've had an extremely positive 18 years (and counting) in the cybersecurity industry. One time when *Infosecurity* was exhibiting at RSA in San Francisco, I was on the booth and asked by a visitor if someone "more senior" was around to talk to, because "I don't have time for booth babes". I very calmly explained I was the Editor and Publisher, so there was no one more senior. I laughed about it afterwards, but really, the audacity and rudeness was shocking. Still, at least I was considered a babe...!

That aside, I've had only positive experiences. I know I'm one of the lucky ones because I've interviewed hundreds of women who have been subject to misogyny, career blocking, disrespect and worse. This industry isn't always a happy place for minorities (which women are in this sector) and

this, I believe, is unforgivable.

*What are the things you've learned being a woman in the cyber security industry?*

I imagine that I've learned a lot of the same things that men have learnt. That said, I've heard interviewees tell me time and time again that they have to achieve way more, learn way more, and try much harder just to be considered an equal to any given man in the sector.

*What advice would you give to women who would like to join the cyber security industry?*

Network to build your tribe. Find industry friends who will raise you up. And have the confidence to know you belong - diversity, quite literally, makes businesses more successful.

*What role does diversity play in cyber security?*

I think this is a very simple answer. People are the most important component of the cybersecurity industry, and diversity is the most important formula for success and prosperity.

*It is widely known that cyber security is still a very male dominated industry, even though it is 2024. Why do you think there are so few women in cyber security?*

Cybersecurity has a marketing issue; the imagery, the rhetoric, the lack of representation. The way the sector is portrayed is dangerous for the industry as it alienates women.

Representation matters, and you can't be what you can't see. Visible role models would go a long way to encouraging more females into the sector. The lack of representation of women in senior roles in the industry is particularly discouraging.

*Who are your role models in cyber security?*

As a journalist, it's frowned upon to have favourites. My list of role models is huge, but for the sake of brevity, I'll choose just one: Katie Moussouris. What. A. Woman!

*If you could go back in time to your first days in the industry, what would you do differently or tell yourself?*

I'd have invested more time in networking early on. I wouldn't have wasted so many years thinking 'I don't deserve to be in this role so young'. And maybe I'd have found my co-founders (Henry and Ed) and launched Assured even sooner... The opportunity we have to improve cyber insurance and give organisations the assurance they deserve really is special, and the difference we're making to our clients is remarkable, and so very rewarding. Plus, we're having the time of our lives doing it!

*If you could give women considering a career in cybersecurity one piece of advice, what would it be?*

Do it. You never regret the chances you take... only the chances you don't take.

*And finally, tell us a few fun things about yourself! Do you have an unusual hobby for example, or a fun fact about yourself that you can share?*

I'm the girliest boy mum, obsessed with my two little men. I love good wine, great books, and even

better holidays. I love to be warm – which is why you'll often find me in front of a log fire, in a hot tub, or on a beach.

I do love to party, but I'm never happier than when I'm in the family nest with my partner and the children. Home is everything!

I'm passionate about telling other people's stories, so telling mine in the answers to these questions feels peculiar.

# Deanna Gibb

**Job Title:** Executive GM - Public Sector

**Company/Organisation:** Willyama Services

*Tell us a bit about your background, your career to date and what you currently do in cyber security.*

Like many of us, I haven't had a traditional pathway into cyber security, although cyber and information security and governance has been a thread throughout my career working in the Australian National Security sector.

I have been spoiled enough to work as both the client and a trusted advisor across all aspects of ICT delivery, operations and sustainment both in Industry and Public Sector. I have traversed technical and business roles and been a key conduit between the two, especially in large business transformation initiatives sitting within Government.

Throughout my career, my focus is always the empowerment of people and organisations to achieve outcomes. I look through the lenses of capability, security, efficiency and strategic mission, drawing on diverse perspectives and tools and an extensive network.

Currently, as the Executive GM for the Public Sector, a key part of my role is leading a team of cyber security professionals in ensuring supply chain security for a large, complex Government client. My remit includes providing strategic advice to help the client frame out their cyber security initiatives, explore policy relevant to their mission, and support the uplift of their cyber security program.

*How did you get into the field of cyber security?*

When I started working in roles that we would now class as cyber security, cyber security didn't exist as a discipline. . . So, in many ways, I have been in cyber security since the early 90s!

I didn't make a transition formally into cyber security until several years ago when I had an epiphany that I was in fact leading and solutioning cyber projects, business cases and strategies through my role in business transformation and it was pointed out to me that I was in fact the pre-eminent SME in that domain.

So, as is my want I took to that with gusto and completed some formal certifications and officially embraced that I was a cyber security professional with expert level experience.

Ironically it wasn't long after that that I found myself in front of 200 people explaining why identity governance and administration was cool. . . and realised that perhaps

I really was a cyber person after all.

*What are the main challenges you've encountered as a woman in cyber security, and how did you overcome them?*

In many ways, I have the people working in cyber security to be the most accepting and inclusive I have encountered. As an environment I have felt more valued, and more respected than in any other aspect of ICT and than I have at any other point in my career. I have actually found that once our respective superpowers and shared passion are established, true cyber geeks are the most accepting of me as a full human being.

That said, as a woman in cyber, I often feel I need to work harder to establish credibility, that I need to over emphasise my age and experience (at the risk of engaging ageism!), and I do still regularly find myself subjected to "hepeating" (when him repeating what you said suddenly makes it valuable), mansplaining, and an assumption that because I am "good at humans" that I can't possibly also be good at the technical.

While my team has a higher representation of women than most, I have often found myself in meetings as the only female. There is still backlash directed at women and an assumption that if I am direct or engaged in a conversation that I am angry, shrill, or bossy, and that I should defer to the men in the discussion - even if I am the most experienced or are their peer.

Interestingly that's not just an attitude I see in men.

I'm also expected to be more capable, more organised, more "perfect" and held to a higher standard than my peers. I overcome this by knowing the matter/situation/

strategy/content in detail (again, I know the data inside and out!). I opt to lift the people around me up to the standard and pace that I want our team to operate at and am deliberate in harnessing the skills and talents and strengths of the fabulous humans I work with.

Sadly, it does still seem that women transitioning into cyber security need to step down to step up (something I have needed to do). I would love to see a day when that is not required.

*What are the things you've learned being a woman in the cyber security industry?*

I have learned that continuous learning is not just a joy but a necessity; that there is a space for every single one of the skills and differences I bring; that when you find your tribe they will lift you up, and inspire you; that if your interest is problem solving, you'll never run out of interesting work to do; that the human side and understanding how to make cyber security relatable, normalised and personal is and will be a key (and your super power too!) to keeping ourselves, our community and our nation secure.

No matter how good your technical skills are, the rate of change of the threat environment and the technology and human's use of it, means that what you've done before is just a building block and you need to re-learn each time there is a step change across the cyber security industry.

*What advice would you give to women who would like to join the cyber security industry?*

You need to understand and then articulate the story of why your transferrable skills are relevant in cyber security. Your skills are more valuable to the cyber security industry than you think. Identify how your skills relate and tell this story (over and over again until you truly believe it and own it!).

Only you can make the links, because only you know why they are relevant. Once you build the connections, and can tell your story, you will be embraced.

Build yourself a network, get involved and follow discussions online around cyber security and technology. Connect with the ASWN, follow AISA, follow social media profiles of female leaders in cyber security. Get involved in hackathons and take part in desktop security incident exercises and teaming, take up the cyber best practices like strong passwords, MFA and patching your own

devices. Get engaged in the doing... so you have the experience! Once you build your connections and get involved you will be able to define where your interests lie. From there, you'll be able to get the qualifications you truly want and are passionate about.

*What role does diversity play in cyber security?*

I recently spoke at CyberCon in Melbourne about my views on diversity in cyber security, and I described it as the Shield Against Cyber Risk! In a future that is fundamentally unknowable and unpredictable how do we protect ourselves, our businesses, our communities from cyber risk? As the threat landscape evolves, so do the strategies and tactics needed to combat cyber risks. So how do we, as a society, as an industry, respond?

In my view it is time to unleash the shield that is diversity, and harness a truly diverse cyber workforce that brings together different perspectives, experiences, and cognitive abilities!

Diverse teams consider a broader range of factors, leading to more comprehensive risk assessments and informed decision-making in the face of cyber threats. Diversity has a pivotal role to play in cyber security, as does leaders learning how to truly lead them and amplify the superpower that is diversity!

*It is widely known that cyber security is still a very male dominated industry, even though it is 2024. Why do you think there are so few women in cyber security?*

If my opinions are dismissed or if my input isn't valued, if I am not allowed to feel like I fit, why would I stay? Cyber doesn't just have a problem with attracting women, it has a problem with retention. Because there are still cultural norms that we need to shift.

You need to have thick skin, a strong sense of confidence in your own skills and judgement, and the tenacity and grit to feel like an outsider, to stay long enough in cyber to find your tribe. And it can be a lonely journey getting there, especially for those of us who have other differences like neurodivergence, disability or a different cultural or work background.

The challenges women face in the workforce exist elsewhere, they are certainly not solely in the prevail of cyber, but there are other areas where it is less overt and where it may be easier to use and be embraced for the skills and strengths you have – or sit down and blend in. But the risk is you get comfortable or die a little inside every day!

So back to the question of why so few women in cyber? I think it's a historical issue largely, that is diminishing.

But until we reach a critical mass, until there are enough women in cyber celebrated and enough ladders out there for women to climb we will retain the imbalance and perception of being an undesirable place for women.

*Who are your role models in cyber security?*

**Kylie Watson - DXC Partner** who has transitioned across roles and domains in a similar way to myself, is an extraordinary leader, focused on the human side of cyber as well as the 'sexy' technology and who has been an amazing mentor and friend to me.

**Rachel Noble - ASD** well duh!!! She leads one of the most important organisations for our nation!!!

**Ricki Burke** I know this sounds odd in an article about women in cyber and I am sure he will be immensely shocked to find this out but... Ricki Burke, the founder of CyberSec People is and continues to be a role model for me as someone who is passionate about the growth of humans, increasing the diversity in cyber and in highlighting and supporting the amazing strengths the neurodivergent bring to our industry.

*If you could go back in time to your first days in the industry, what would you do differently or tell yourself?*

In my first days in the industry, I relied heavily on being told I "do Cyber Security" but I didn't feel it in my bones. There was this irritating and completely inaccurate internal narrative I told myself that I wasn't technical enough, that I wasn't good enough. BUT IN REALITY was I knew far more than I allowed myself credit! So, if I step into the Tardis (Dr Who, anyone?!) and go back to my first "official" cyber security foray, I would say to myself:

*You've been building systems using the principles of security by design and zero trust before those terms were coined. Trust your judgement. Learn how to use the terminology. And go for it... because you've got this! And don't underestimate how much you do know, how technical you really are and how much your true delight in solving problems will be key to your success.*

*Your understanding and ability to connect with humans in a logical and empathetic way is far more valuable that you believe. Don't ever lose that.*

*And whatever you do, bring your whole self, and don't sit down!!!!*

I'm not saying that would have made the path any easier but those are the messages I needed to hear and that I tell my people every day.

*If you could give women considering a career in cybersecurity one piece of advice, what would it be?*

Find the part of cyber security that ignites your passion! Whether that be - your creative side, your hyper focus, your systematic, logical, analytical attention to detail, your blue sky thinking, your love of a good crisis or your love of stability... find the place in cyber that ignites you! This will then be self-sustaining, you will find the right spot, and you will never doubt why you came!

When you find the places where people all fit, they really thrive, and there is a place in cyber security for everyone.

# Laurie Gibbett

**Job Title:** Cyber Risk Quantification Manager

**Company/Organisation:** KPMG

*Tell us a bit about your background, your career to date and what you currently do in cyber security.*

I started my career in the cyber security industry in 2016 as a security specialist, supporting senior cybersecurity consultants with their engagements, client workshops and competitive bids. I soon moved into a business role to set-up a bid and proposal practice, supporting the security team with competitive proposals. As I learned more about cybersecurity, I moved away from helping internal teams alone, to directly helping organisations reduce their cyber risk. This enabled me to move into cyber strategy and risk consulting in 2020. I enjoy helping organisations understand, measure, and reduce their cyber risk exposure through effective control strategies. Today I help organisations make more informed decisions on managing cyber risk through the adoption of cyber risk quantification.

*How did you get into the field of cyber security?*

It wasn't planned, it was the unknown. I wasn't sure what I wanted to do as a career. I pursued a degree in Business Studies to give me a breadth of skills that could be applied in many fields. I started my career initially in consumer marketing, but after moving to a business-to-business role, I learned about the opportunities in cybersecurity. There was always something going on and always something new to learn, which is exciting. I was able to move to the industry because of the rotation option on the graduate scheme and I haven't left since.

*What are the main challenges you've encountered as a woman in cyber security, and how did you overcome them?*

I personally don't feel there is a barrier me being in the industry because I'm a woman. I try to embody this mindset and encourage others to consider adopting a positive attitude. There is no doubt there are many individuals who have unfortunately had negative experiences accentuated by their gender. We must work together as a community to understand the problems and put actions in place to stop them. We must start with awareness. If we are not sharing these experiences and including male advocates as part of our community, they will not be well understood or addressed.

*What advice would you give to women who would like to join the cyber security industry?*

Diversity is critical for the industry's success. There are so many specialised areas, cyber threats, industries to protect, a one-size-fits-all approach isn't effective. How can we as teams think differently, innovate, adapt, if we have the same skills and interests. Also, there is still a need for business roles in cyber security. Burnout is a real thing in this industry. We need a good support system of supportive management and human resources. Vendors need marketeers, sales, product managers. There's a role for everyone.

*If you could go back in time to your first days in the industry, what would you do differently or tell yourself?*

I started in the industry as a graduate and although I don't regret the experiences I had, if I could go back in time, I would encourage myself to take on more experiences across other cyber domain areas. Being a graduate, you have a safe space to work on a variety of engagements and build your knowledge through training. If you get that kind of opportunity, you should absolutely make the most of it. Help yourself by helping others and staying curious.

*If you could give women considering a career in cybersecurity one piece of advice, what would it be?*

Go for it! Everyone has something to bring to the table and the industry needs diversity. There are a lot of routes into the industry and if you're reading interviews like this, you already have one stream of help, us! Cybersecurity has many domain areas of specialism, so it can help if you have an idea of where you want to go from a training perspective. But it's also ok to start broad and specialise later. Many of us have.

*And finally, tell us a few fun things about yourself! Do you have an unusual hobby for example, or a fun fact about yourself that you can share?*

I live on the North Devon coast with my two ragdoll cats Ragnar and Floki. For those that have seen it, yes, they're named after the characters from Vikings. I'm often found on the river Torridge as late 2023 I got into gig rowing. Although I'm relatively new to the sport I've been taking it seriously and on track to compete at the World Gig Rowing Championships at the Isles of Scillies this spring.

# Wendy Goucher

**Job Title:** Cyber Security Consultant

**Company/Organisation:** Arcanum Cyber

*Tell us a bit about your background, your career to date and what you currently do in cyber security.*

I trained as a teacher and lecturer and worked as a management lecturer in FE, HE and University for over 20 years. Moved because I needed a challenge and was ready for a change. For the past few years I have found my feet working in Risk and Assurance where I can use a range of my tech-less abilities. I have also written a few books; some text books but also some cyber safety books for young children and short (ish) stories for senior folk.

*How did you get into the field of cyber security?*

Info Sec community (still is) and he suggested that Information Security needed a management perspective.

*What are the main challenges you've encountered as a woman in cyber security, and how did you overcome them?*

My biggest challenge is I am neurodivergent which means I can't sit exams so I can't gain professional qualifications. My MSc is by research and my teaching qualification was by continuous assessment and school was a nightmare. When I was an independent consultant it was very difficult to pick up contracts because of this issue.

*What are the things you've learned being a woman in the cyber security industry?*

The power of being part of a team that share similar challenges. Having someone beside you who has real insight into working around the attitudes others take into evaluating me because I am neurodivergent or female or both is something that was a revelation to me as for a long time I preferred working around men.

*What advice would you give to women who would like to join the cyber security industry?*

Take the time, and speak to others to help you build a picture of who you are and what you can bring to the profession. If you know yourself it is easier to withstand the misperceptions of others

*What role does diversity play in cyber security?*

I believe it is a challenge and a gift. In the next 10 to 15 years the nature of diversity will change as the profession slowly identifies the gifts that the diverse groups can bring. Most importantly diversity teaches us that knowing and being ourselves in our abilities as well as challenges makes a more effective profession - especially when it is a profession that thrives on problem solving and 'thinking outside of the box'.

*It is widely known that cyber security is still a very male dominated industry, even though it is 2024. Why do you think there are so few women in cyber security?*

There are more tech women than there used to be, though not enough, but what the profession needs is to make better use of the insight and skills that are often dismissed as 'soft skills' such as communication and management.

*Who are your role models in cyber security?*

I am not a person who looks at role models, mostly because they always make me feel inferior. How can I even aspire to be like you, Lisa, or Holly Foxcroft or Lianne Potter - what a bunch of amazing ladies. I will never be as good in cyber security as them and knowing this makes me feel bad. I have to confess to having applied for a couple of awards to try and promote the cyber safety books for children and the stories for elder folk, but I cringe when I do because when I see people announcing they win things while I am glad for them there is a bit of me that says 'they are so amazing, why do I bother?' I know this is wrong, but a role model for me is a wonderful person who, when I compare myself to them makes me feel rubbish.

*If you could go back in time to your first days in the industry, what would you do differently or tell yourself?*

I would have looked at areas like Risk and Assurance which makes more use of my understanding of business and communications than the Security Awareness work I tried. Not least because, for too long Security Awareness was seen as 'common sense' and not worth investing in so I spent a long time banging my head against a wall. I am delighted that, not least due to the amazing work of Jemma Davis and Lianne Potter, this is changing.

*If you could give women considering a career in cybersecurity one piece of advice, what would it be?*

Get to know yourself with honesty and talk to people in the profession and find where your insights and abilities will best add value.

*And finally, tell us a few fun things about yourself! Do you have an unusual hobby for example, or a fun fact about yourself that you can share?*

I write stuff - cyber and some history. My daftest fact is that on reaching a significant age I decided I should learn to ride a horse. I'm dyspraxic so there are days when not walking into doors is a challenge, but I'm doing it anyway. It is a long process, but learning to work with a horse is a great discipline for me.

I also have been on a couple of acting workshop retreats learning how to be a storyteller in primary schools and how to narrate the stories for seniors into audio books. I am still trying to come to terms with the tech on the latter one. According the acting coach who is hugely respected in the acting world, I am now 'an actor'. Certain I don't feel worthy of that, and it is probably not something I will put on my CV.

# Ellen Hallam

**Job Title:** Senior Threat Intelligence Analyst

**Company/Organisation:** Bytes Software Services

*Tell us a bit about your background, your career to date and what you currently do in cyber security.*

I joined the Intelligence Corps Army Reserves at 18 and still work for them around my day job. The Reserves set me up for life; the pay supported me through university, gave me the experience to apply for my first job and morphed me into the woman I am today. I met my partner through the Reserves and wouldn't have my son if I hadn't been in either! I've supported the Whaley Bridge dam collapse, back in 2019, where I monitored the situation and briefed the commander on the evacuation and relief effort. I also supported the Covid-19 pandemic in 2020, where I analysed local populations to identify vaccination and testing centres, whilst also monitoring other potential risks, such as bird flu!

I joined HMRC as an Intelligence Analyst and worked there for 4 years. I worked on the Organised Crime team and spent a year as an operational analyst, working on covert sources and drawing conclusions from patterns in data. I got promoted and worked on more strategic topics, including new and emerging threats as well as more general revenue threats like tobacco and money laundering. I got promoted again to Senior Analyst, where I led the Repayment Fraud Team in support of HMRC's response to organised criminality within Repayment fraud. I really enjoyed leading a team and building their confidence. I also taught the Government Intelligence Analytical Techniques course, which taught our analysts the basics of intelligence analysis.

I currently work for Bytes Software Services, as their Threat Intelligence Analyst. This job is completely different to any I've had before, as I now work for a private company. Bytes is a software reseller, and I am really enjoying the challenge of tailoring intelligence to a wide range of personas, from Sales, who want to supply intelligence and security products, to the CISO (Chief Information Security Officer), who uses intelligence for budgeting decisions and strategic decision making. I love being able to work with such a wide range of audiences. I also deliver verbal briefings – my most recent one was to a government audience, where I talked about the WannaCry attack and how proactive threat intelligence could have mitigated – and even prevented – the attack. I love how varied my role is and how I can support Bytes both internally, by providing threat assessments and Mitre Att&ck modelling, as well as externally by using intelligence to generate sales and identify gaps in the security market.

*How did you get into the field of cyber security?*

I realised that the future of intelligence, for me, was cyber and really wanted a new challenge, so I left Government and found a job working in the private sector. I keep up with current affairs and felt that every day, new threats were emerging; new methods of extorting people or hacking into our digital lives and this can affect everyone, as we all have a digital footprint in some way. The advent of Artificial Intelligence is accelerating threats at a phenomenal pace as our attack surface is widening. For example, I work from home full time, but that means I need a Virtual Private Network (VPN), or a computer not directly connected to my work systems, to prevent against threat actors pivoting off my machine and into our network, where client data is securely stored.

I also have a young son and am acutely aware of the dangers of the internet. I really want to fight for a better and more secure future for him. I want to grow up with an appreciation of how good technology is, but also a good understanding of the importance of protecting data and being aware of the risks and threats to your online privacy.

*What are the main challenges you've encountered as a woman in cyber security, and how did you overcome them?*

I have two ongoing challenges, which I am constantly overcoming. The first is having a work life balance. I find it difficult to hold down a full-time career and be a Mum too – and I know many of the women I speak to, who are also parents, struggle with this and the associated "Mum guilt" of never doing enough for your children. I overcame this initial challenge by finding a job which is supportive of me and other women, but also by ensuring I have strong mental resilience and the ability to give quality time to my son around work.

Secondly, I've encountered multiple instances of sexism through both Military and Civilian careers. Some examples include inappropriate appearance-related comments from senior soldiers, or cultural differences between countries – I once received training from US contractors who tried to belittle me – and the other young women on the training exercise by making personal comments – who knew that having your hair neatly tied back in plaits, looking like (in their words) "Pippy Longstocking" could affect your operational capability... I overcome this by simply doing my job and in doing that let the facts speak for themselves. I also don't let inappropriate behaviour be ignored and will actively challenge this, through the correct routes.

*What are the things you've learned being a woman in the cyber security industry?*

I've learned that there are frustratingly, very few of us! I've also learned that diversity sometimes does not seem important to everybody – I went to a big event for an industry-leading Threat Intelligence platform. I was frustrated to find they had two panels of white, middle-aged men, without a woman, or ethnically diverse person in sight, though I can name many, myself including, who would happily have been on the panel and capable of discussing the topics mentioned.

I've also learned that we have to fight a lot harder to prove our capability and our worth.

*What advice would you give to women who would like to join the cyber security industry?*

1. Be flexible! I've often found that the job I end up doing is somewhat different from the job I thought I was applying for. Be confident, take it in your stride and use the opportunity to learn.

2. Remember you cannot know everything. Use each day as a learning opportunity.

3. Find an employer who shares your values. Can you see a visible leader, who is inspirational, and you can respect, learn from and who actively encourages inclusivity and individual personalities. This means you can be yourself - and thrive.

*What role does diversity play in cyber security?*

An absolutely vital role! Without diversity, we have group think. Without diversity, we can't think outside the box and consider events from a different perspective. Without diversity, we aren't challenged to think differently, or question ourselves. Our upbringing and lived experiences affect who we are and what we can bring to a team. This is particularly important to me from an intelligence side, as analysts are prone to bias, or can fall foul of fallacies, as we saw with the Iraq enquiry, where circular reporting contributed to the decision to go to war. I can think of numerous times, where someone from a different background to me has thought about a problem from a different angle. This is particularly useful when 'red teaming' and trying to think like the enemy would – as the enemy has different values and experiences, meaning they may place importance on things we would not necessarily consider with a typical "white, middle-class background."

I think Bytes, for example, not only recognise the value of diversity, but actively encourage it. I work with a plethora of ethnically diverse people, which brings new thought processes and ways of doing things. I also love learning about new culture's – one lady who I get on with well, has a Pakistani heritage and I was thrilled as she gave me cooking herbs and spices so I could make a delicious curry! Bytes also realised that their Parental policy did not encourage parents to stay working for Bytes after their Maternity/Paternity leave, so they now have one of the best Parental leave policies I have seen, which again encourages diversity and makes parents feel included too!

*It is widely known that cyber security is still a very male dominated industry, even though it is 2024. Why do you think there are so few women in cyber security?*

I believe that this stems from education and that we are not encouraging young girls to study Sciences, Technology, Engineering or Maths (STEM subjects) enough. I think there is a perception that Cyber is "not cool" and that it conforms to a specific social stereotype, or that you have to excel at Computer Science, algorithms or maths to be able to have a successful career.

Having come from an Intelligence background, which lends itself more, perhaps to English and writing skills, I also don't feel the breadth of roles available is fully explored or broadcast in schools. Nor do I feel the path to a job in Cyber is as delineated as a job in Medicine, or teaching two give two examples of careers, or vocations with clear development pathways and "contained" options. The plethora of roles available in Cyber are confusing and technical. Irrespective, we need more women in Cyber to combat stereotypes and the status quo.

*Who are your role models in cyber security?*

I have 3:

1. I had one role model, who still inspires me today. She commissioned into the Intelligence Corps Reserves and inspired me when I was a young and naïve 20-year-old. I remember going to visit the LIFC (Land Intelligence Fusion Cell), who collate intelligence and disseminate products for the Army and wider interested parties. This woman – Lauren Phipps, delivered a 45-minute brief on the Islamic State, with no notes, in front of several hundred people. She was an absolute inspiration, intelligent, motivated and encouraging. She did a tour of Iraq and developed breast cancer when she came back. She fought it off once, not missing a single day of work (she worked for the Salvation Army), but I was devastated to learn that the cancer regressed, and she passed away in April 2021. I frequently ask myself, "What would Lauren do?"

2. My second role model is another Officer in the Intelligence Corps Reserves. She works in Cyber and holds down her Reserve career, a full-time day job for financial services and is a wife, and a Mum to two young boys. She is always available to chat, is approachable, understanding and down to earth. I love that we have an affinity and understanding, through

shared struggles and shared experiences. When I was pregnant, she helped me feel empowered to understand the policy around pregnancy and breastfeeding, and actively helped my unit understand what I needed to do and what I was entitled to (as I was the first woman in my unit to be pregnant.) I even managed to go on an arduous Leadership training course, with 5 days of exercise in the field, whilst expressing milk!

3. Your role-models do not have to be women – Inclusive leaders, regardless of gender, can be role-models to everybody. I also have a male role-model, who is the Vice President of a well-known Security solutions platform. This man made the effort to come across London to meet me; we have regular catch-up conversations, and he is a font of Cyber knowledge. I love the discussions we have and how approachable and encouraging he is. I am open and frank with him and I know he respects me for that!

*If you could go back in time to your first days in the industry, what would you do differently or tell yourself?*

I'd tell myself that it is impossible for you to know everything or be good at everything. Every day is a learning day, and I would go back and challenge myself to write down something new I learnt, every day, so I could track my progress. I'd also tell myself to think outside the box even more and trust my instincts.

*If you could give women considering a career in cybersecurity one piece of advice, what would it be?*

Find a mentor and surround yourself with people who empower you. Linked In is brilliant for connecting with people (especially after you've been to women in cyber events and met other successful and soon to be successful women), so use this to your advantage and find your group. I'd also say, think about what you want to achieve every day and in every meeting. If you don't get the desired outcome, don't give up and keep trying until you do.

*And finally, tell us a few fun things about yourself! Do you have an unusual hobby for example, or a fun fact about yourself that you can share?*

I speak Spanish, I love knitting and crochet (and I'm currently teaching myself Tunisian Crochet). I play piano and I do agility with my Border Collie!

Fun fact: I appeared in an episode of Bargain Hunt... We were the blue team and we lost...!

# Amelia Hewitt

**Job Title:** Cyber Security Consultant/Director

**Company/Organisation:** Hewitt Partnerships Ltd

*Tell us a bit about your background, your career to date and what you currently do in cyber security.*

I started my career as an IT Apprentice in the Legal sector, and after a secondment into the Cyber team, I found that the parts of the job I loved in my IT role such as collaborating with others and finding solutions were the fundamental elements of a Cyber consulting career. I quickly made the jump to Cyber consulting, and have spent my career since then working with Critical National Infrastructure clients to implement Cyber Security and Data Protection frameworks. In 2023, I became self-employed, and have since worked within the private sector, providing Cyber Advisory services to a range of industries.

*How did you get into the field of cyber security?*

Cyber was never my 'dream' career, but I was proactive and passionate in getting exposure in my first role into the world of Cyber, and utilised that secondment experience, alongside my experience in IT to land my first consulting role. I had never formally studied IT prior to my apprenticeship, so I used the same 'learn as you go' mindset to build my Cyber career.

*What are the main challenges you've encountered as a woman in cyber security, and how did you overcome them?*

Throughout my journey as a woman in cyber security, I have encountered adversity, yet these challenges have undeniably honed my professional ability. Early in my career, I grappled with issues of credibility, especially in a client-facing role. This manifested in many ways, including being overlooked or interrupted in meetings, and witnessing my deliverables being attributed to others. As a result, I felt compelled to continuously validate my expertise and worth, which over time, became exhausting. However, over the course of my career, I have adopted a more strategic approach, allowing the quality of my work to speak for my competence. I have also built assertiveness, which has come with building both confidence and experience to ensure that my contributions receive the recognition and respect they deserve.

Additionally, working in Cyber as a minority has magnified feelings of imposter syndrome. Despite having a sufficient portfolio of experience, moments of self-doubt and questioning my rightful place among more senior professionals, still occasionally surface. To address this, I have been intentionally refining my internal dialogue and the manner in which I articulate my professional narrative. For example, rather than saying 'I have been lucky to have been given opportunity', I now say 'I have worked hard to explore opportunities, and grateful for the support I've had'. This subtle yet profound shift in self-perception and communication has significantly reduced the feelings of imposter syndrome, as I am giving myself more credit for my achievements, rather than attributing them to luck.

*What are the things you've learned being a woman in the cyber security industry?*

One of the most invaluable lessons I've embraced as a woman in the cyber security field is the critical role of community. Cultivating a network filled with diverse professionals has not only inspired me immensely, but also provided a robust support system throughout my career. This network has been instrumental in enabling me to navigate various professional hurdles, fostering my growth both as an individual and as a professional. Also, I have learned the significance of establishing boundaries—a lesson particularly important in the context of being a woman in Cyber. This awareness has empowered me to identify workplace practices and behaviours that do not align with my values and to effectively communicate my limits to colleagues.

Reflecting on my journey, the obstacles I've encountered in the cyber security industry have actually served as pivotal learning opportunities. These experiences have deepened my understanding of myself, reinforcing my resilience and adaptability, and provided me with the experience I need to support others in similar positions.

*What advice would you give to women who would like to*

*join the cyber security industry?*

The biggest piece of advice I give to early-stage professionals is to 'Just enjoy it'. There is so much pressure to build a career, or reach a specific 'end goal' position, and that can often take up so much of our energy, that we forget to enjoy the time we spend getting there. I know from personal experience that treating a career in Cyber as a sprint leads to significant burn-out, so I'd encourage women who'd like to join Cyber to rid themselves of those expectations, and really take time to understand themselves as professionals, rather than rushing to meet a goal. It builds much healthier, sustainable habits which lead to longer-term retention of women in Cyber.

*What role does diversity play in cyber security?*

As a woman in cyber, I've observed firsthand how varied perspectives enhance problem-solving capabilities and foster innovative solutions to complex security challenges. In an ever-evolving threat landscape, diversity in thought, background, and experience is key to staying proactive as a sector.

I believe that diversity is instrumental in addressing the cyber talent gap. By embracing inclusivity, the industry can tap into a broader talent pool, mitigating workforce shortages and enhancing capabilities. It also encourages a culture of continuous learning and adaptability, crucial traits for staying ahead in a field marked by rapid technological advancements.

*It is widely known that cyber security is still a very male dominated industry, even though it is 2024. Why do you think there are so few women in cyber security?*

There are several factors that contribute to this. I have first-hand witnessed how the education system contributes to a lack of women in Cyber. The UK education system, through various structural and cultural elements, inadvertently deters girls from pursuing STEM (Science, Technology, Engineering, Mathematics) subjects. This deterrence often stems from early education experiences, where gender stereotypes and biases subtly influence the participation of girls in STEM-related activities and subjects. These stereotypes can manifest in classroom dynamics, teacher expectations, and the availability of role models, which collectively may lead girls to perceive STEM as less welcoming or suitable for them. The underrepresentation of women in STEM fields at the educational level directly translates into the workforce, including the cyber security sector.

Additionally, issues surrounding the retention of women in Cyber play a key role in the statistics that portray Cyber as male-dominated. Cyber security, like many STEM fields, can have a male-dominated culture that may not be inclusive or supportive of women. This environment can lead to feelings of isolation, lack of belonging, or encountering gender biases. Also, women may face overt or subtle discrimination in the workplace, including wage gaps, being overlooked for promotions, or not being taken as seriously as their male colleagues, especially if they decide to take a career break in order to support a family. Such experiences can diminish job motivation to stay in the field. Both factors have been widely understood to impact attrition rates for women in Cyber, and must be dealt with to ensure that we are able to retain female talent in the sector.

With both factors in mind, it is easy to see how the lack

of women in Cyber is a systemic issue.

*Who are your role models in cyber security?*

I haven't necessarily had role models over the course of my career, which is mostly a personal observation, as my career hasn't followed a conventional path. However, I have surrounded myself with a diverse range of professionals, both male and female, to ensure that I get a breadth of influence.

*If you could go back in time to your first days in the industry, what would you do differently or tell yourself?*

If I could revisit my early career, I would not necessarily do anything differently, as I believe that my experiences have led me to my current career, and a place where I am comfortable and content. However, I would want to tell my former self to enjoy where I am, rather than forcing so much pressure upon myself to reach the next step so quickly. There has been so much value in taking my professional life at a slower pace, and I would have liked to have understood this sooner.

*If you could give women considering a career in cybersecurity one piece of advice, what would it be?*

There are so many great answers to this, but most importantly, I'd encourage women considering a career in Cyber to embrace your unique perspective and be secure in the knowledge of what you bring to the industry, be it technical or interpersonal skills. Women bring invaluable insights and skills to the table, which are essential for innovating and navigating the complex security challenges we face as an industry. Feeling secure in how you bring a diverse perspective provides a multitude of benefits such as enhanced confidence within application processes, assertiveness when faced with adversity, and subsequently, a much happier career.

*And finally, tell us a few fun things about yourself! Do you have an unusual hobby for example, or a fun fact about yourself that you can share?*

Perhaps not too fun, but I adore a challenge, which most often manifests as a very busy schedule! I started a Bsc Combined STEM degree as a hobby, and I love spending time finding new projects and ideas to get stuck into.

# Bishakha Jain

**Job Title:** Manager, Cyber Data Risk and Resiliance

**Company/Organisation:** Morgan Stanley

*Tell us a bit about your background, your career to date and what you currently do in cyber security.*

I am Bishakha Jain, a cyber security evangelist from India. I have a demonstrated history across multiple security domains through my various years of experience in the Cyber Security industry. Academically, I am an engineer, an MBA and a cyber law graduate on papers. I have a rich history in working with various communities across the globe and I am passionate about increasing diversity participation in Cybersecurity and have trained over 25K plus diverse candidates which includes Army Veterans, Police candidates, children,graduate and post graduate students and Executive Professionals. I currently work for Morgan Stanley India, heading their Cyber Risk Awareness and Business Intelligence competency for India. I am responsible for managing all aspects of the Firm's anti-phishing program. My role is to ensure business unit support and reporting in region and broadly as needed across the lifecycle of campaign cycles and as required by phishing risk and risk mitigation efforts.

*How did you get into the field of cyber security?*

My entry in the world of cyber security was all things serendipity. Let's say the universe has been sending me signals about the destiny since my engineering days. During the fifth semester of my engineering, we used to have a subject called "Computer Networks" and the naughty student that I used to be was caught playing cross and dots in the first lecture. My Professor then asked me to teach the Chapter on Cryptographic concepts the next day to the entire class as a punishment. I was out of choice, I had to study the subject for the presentation next day in front of the entire class. But to my amazement I started loving the subject and in no time Alice and Bob (the famous cryptographic characters) became my best friends. And eventually I landed in my first job as a penetration tester, those concepts came easy to me as I developed my affinity towards the same since my early graduation days. And then it was during my first job that a Mentor of mine suggested that I should try my luck in an MBA in Cybersecurity, I liked the idea of taking a break for higher education and thereafter I was hired by IBM during my campus placements and everything else is a glorious history. I met some of the most passionate people during my stint at IBM, Lisa Venture being one of them. They opened doors for me in ways I never imagined. There are synergies in the field that I explored during those 3 years of service which led to my career progression ahead. And I am still exploring, and like Robert Frost once said, "And miles to go before I sleep."

*What are the main challenges you've encountered as a woman in cyber security, and how did you overcome them?*

Honestly, I consider myself very fortunate to have such a strong support system and advocates in the industry. However, there's always another side of the story that we go through so that we can grow through. I have had people take away my credits for the work done. There were days when burning outs was normalised. But I believe there's always a choice, the only things that makes the difference is what do we choose. I chose to call out misuse of my work which I do realise is not always the smartest thing to do. I chose to change paths from people and projects which no longer served my purpose and my wellbeing. Because I vehemently believe you cannot pour from an empty cup, so over these years of my service I have learnt to make sure that my cup runneth over so that I can contribute passionately to the global cyber security community.

*What are the things you've learned being a woman in the cyber security industry?*

Being a woman in the cyber security industry the learnings were many. Let's try bringing them to book(laughs). I learnt that there's nothing wrong in not knowing something but being ignorant is not the solution. In Charlie Munger's words "Acknowledging what you don't know is the dawning of wisdom." In our industry talent is overrated but "Resilience" is super underrated but it's the temperament that makes all the difference not the unused intellect. I have also learnt approaching the problems with the Feynman technique which is based around the idea that one of the most effective techniques to enhance our understanding is to imagine that we're teaching the material to someone who has absolutely no idea about the topic. Like a small child. Because I believe simplicity is the ultimate sophistication and getting the basics right makes one an accomplished Cyber Security Expert with a strong foundation in fundamentals. Another learning that I have imbibed is that if someone opens a door of opportunity for me, it's my responsibility that I pass on the privilege to other women and not be a doorkeeper.

*What advice would you give to women who would like to join the cyber security industry?*

A piece of advice that I would like to give to women who would like to join the cyber security industry is that you are diving in an ocean of opportunities, don't shy away in exploring the avenues this behemoth field has to offer. You can be anything you want to be (here and in life), never stop believing. Remember learning is a lifelong process, dream big and never settle. Find Mentors and sponsors for progressing in your career and always giveback.

*What role does diversity play in cyber security?*

Diversity is a gift in cyber security. Kindling different perspective through diverse candidates can help in identifying and addressing security risks that might not be apparent to a more homogenous group. Diverse teams are better equipped to think outside the box and come up with unconventional approaches to security challenges. Different individuals bring different skill sets to the table. By fostering diversity, cybersecurity teams can access a broader range of expertise enabling more effective and efficient responses to security incidents It's about building stronger, more resilient teams that are better equipped to tackle the complex and ever-evolving challenges in the cybersecurity landscape.

*It is widely known that cyber security is still a very male dominated industry, even though it is 2024. Why do you think there are so few women in cyber security?*

There are many reasons behind the less representation. Some of them that I feel are reluctance to claim their achievements downplaying their accomplishments and hesitating to take credit for the work. This leads to lesser women in the leadership by climbing up the ladder. Not leveraging the connections effectively to advance the career rather always focusing on building new relationships is another reason. The scarcity of visible female role models in cybersecurity can make it difficult for young women to envision themselves pursuing careers in the field. Without relatable figures to emulate, it's challenging for girls to see cybersecurity as a viable and welcoming career option.

*Who are your role models in cyber security?*

I believe in taking inspiration from everything around me and I have had many Mentors in the industry who have walked me through various phases of my career. Everyone had some lessons to impart which kept me rolling relevantly over the years.

*If you could go back in time to your first days in the industry, what would you do differently or tell yourself?*

I would advise my younger self to learn to say NO wherever necessary.

*If you could give women considering a career in cybersecurity one piece of advice, what would it be?*

Here's my golden lesson: Learning is a lifelong process; Ideas rule the world and Knowledge is Power. Keep exploring and let this field surprise you.

*And finally, tell us a few fun things about yourself! Do you have an unusual hobby for example, or a fun fact about yourself that you can share?*

There's more to my life than Cybersecurity. I love reading and travelling. I am a self-taught painter and I plan to sell my art someday. I also can cook very well. And I love hosting parties at my home. I love writing poems. Basically, I live to explore and learning a new hobby has always been my leisure pursuits.

# Bandana Kaur

**Job Title:** Ethical Hacker

**Company/Organisation:** High School (11th Grade)

*Tell us a bit about your background, your career to date and what you currently do in cyber security.*

From playgrounds to Kali Linux, curiosity led me here and then there was no turning back. After an adverse experience on social media, Python became my second language at 13. My first personal project was the creation of a voice-automated zoom bot that joined online classes for

103

me in 2020. That marked the beginning of my love story with Computer Programming and Cybersecurity. Competitive Programming became my happy place; on platforms like GeeksForGeeks, CodeChef and HackerRank where I hold Certifications in Python and SQL. Then came the internship under FutureReadyTalent and Microsoft, where I wasn't just learning, I was building - a network monitoring tool. I'm an ISC2 Certified Cybersecurity professional and a Cisco Certified Ethical Hacker

So, what do I currently do? I'm almost in the 12th grade and preparing for university admission exams. To fuel my own interest and passion, I'm a CTF player on TryHackMe and HackTheBox, and a Cybersecurity Career Ambassador for NICE. My thirst for knowledge led me to Harvard Online's Python and AI courses, where I'm currently diving into the fascinating world of machine learning. But what describes me best would be my undying love for cybersecurity.

But hold on, this story is not all about me. I know the biggest barrier to this field isn't technical, it's the intimidating perception of cybersecurity that has been created by stereotypes in pop culture. That's why I launched "HackWitHer," where I believe in Hacking the Mindset to learn and master the toughest of cybersecurity topics. Having studied for the CC and CEH exams, I break down complex concepts, making cybersecurity accessible to everyone. Why? Because I believe anyone can get into cyber security, with the right mindset and passion.

I believe the biggest vulnerability isn't technical, it's the gap between potential and purpose. And I'm here to contribute in whatever way I can to bridge that gap, one line of code, one conquered CTF challenge, one empowered individual at a time.

*How did you get into the field of cyber security?*

My journey in cybersecurity was very unconventional, and fueled by a personal experience. Like many people, I joined social media at a very young age and had an online encounter that made me realize the importance of digital safety. That's when I decided I was going to fight back and contribute to the safety of our cyberworld, so that nobody has to go through the same things I did. Python became my friend at 13, and I poured my energy into learning it.

Seeing a young woman lead a hacker group in 'Salvation', while mastering both AI and cybersecurity, ignited a passion within me. At 14, I was a CTF Player on TryHackMe, starting in the domain of Open Source Intelligence. It was fascinating to me how someone's digital footprint could be traced by their online presence. Now, I've moved to Penetration Testing and AI. While this fictional character on Netflix did inspire me, She can't compare to the incredible women i met on Linkedin. These connections proved far more powerful than any fictional character.

But what really drives me is passion. It's not just about the technical aspects; it's about the thrill in the challenge, the puzzle, the constant learning. My Kali LInux machine is my happy place.

I believe the best thing, by far, that I have done in the 2-3 years I spent learning Cybersecurity is my most recent venture -'HackWitHer', where I explain concepts in ways that helped my teenage mind understand them. Through this, I've been able to give back to the community that welcomed me with open arms. Now, I want to use my knowledge to inspire others who might think cybersecurity is out of reach.

*What are the main challenges you've encountered as a woman in cyber security, and how did you overcome them?*

When you love something like cybersecurity as deeply as I did, as early as 14, of course there are challenges.

While my loved ones didn't actively discourage me, navigating this field independently, without readily available mentors, peers or guidance, presented its own challenges. Some days I would be in an absolute frenzy because I felt highly unorganized. To declutter my mind, I started journaling.

The best piece of advice that I ever got was that the trivial 15-20 things on my to-do list were my biggest distractions against the top 5.

I also struggled with low self-esteem; That's when I discovered the power of self-belief. I only kept doing what I love the most; and eventually, that love found its way back to me. I learned to fall in love with the journey and trust my own instincts.

I wish I could say 'One magical day, there were no challenges', but I would be lying. While the challenges continue, I embrace them as opportunities to learn and grow. The journey may not always be conventional, but the satisfaction of pursuing my passion and contributing to the cybersecurity community makes it all worthwhile.

*What are the things you've learned being a woman in the cyber security industry?*

The biggest thing I've learned being in this industry is that your "why's" are your superpower.

For most of my academic life, this question of mine made me stand out, sometimes uncomfortably. I wasn't just satisfied with surface-level knowledge; I craved understanding the root cause. This could be frustrating for teachers and peers, but in the world of cybersecurity, it became my superpower. My relentless "why's" became the foundation of my analytical thinking and problem-solving skills when it comes to cybersecurity.

Beyond the technical aspects, cybersecurity has helped me conquer my social anxiety. With practice and support from the community, I've gained confidence in my voice and ability to connect with others. This has been incredibly rewarding, both personally and professionally.

I don't know where exactly I'm headed, but I do know how I started, and I'm very proud of myself for having made it this far without giving up on myself, and will keep doing what i love most. Looking ahead, I'm excited to keep learning, growing, and contributing to a more inclusive cybersecurity space.

*What advice would you give to women who would like to join the cyber security industry?*

"In this field there is only a good learner and a great learner. The moment that you become a great learner is when you become a cybersecurity professional."

This statement of mine holds a special place in my heart, as being a continuous learner and patient with myself was something I once struggled with.

Cybersecurity is all about being a lifelong student - not just when it comes to technical concepts. It's about nurturing the art of effective communication, networking and gratitude, which is more rewarding than it sounds! There will be times when learning that Imposter Syndrome will whisper doubts in your ear, but never undermine yourself, or underestimate your own potential. You are capable of anything you set your mind to and that if you are passionate enough about something, nothing can stop you from mastering the most complicated of topics. As they say, fall in love with the journey, not just the destination.

Some more actionable advice would be to start working the job before you get the job.

What I mean by that is if you want to be an OSINT Analyst, start conducting OSINT investigations on your own accounts, and document that process. This can also mean using the Feynman Technique - Demonstrate and solidify your knowledge of cybersecurity by teaching somebody!

In cybersecurity, there's no finish line when it comes to learning.

*What role does diversity play in cyber security?*

Do you know about the North Indian concept of "jugaad"? It's a slang word which means solving complex problems with resourcefulness and creative workarounds. In the 80s, someone made "Water Walking Shoes" using thermocol so people could commute easily in rural areas where waterlogging was a common problem, his invention is still being used to this day. Creative right?

How does this relate to diversity in cybersecurity? Imagine the sort of innovation that could take place in the field of cybersecurity when the voices of people from backgrounds with such promising cultural ideals are heard.

Modern cybersecurity problems need diverse solutions. Think of Pandora's box. It's said to contain dangers and horrors that may as well destroy the world. What if it was guarded by only one type of lock? This lock on pandora's box is a metaphor for our cybersecurity professionals guarding us against the horrors of cybercrime. Creativity isn't enough to combat next-generation cybercrime, we also need diverse perspectives. Reasoning, problem solving abilities and thought processes depend heavily on a person's physical, regional, and mental background.

We don't just need diversity to fill quotas, we need variety in mindsets as our Pandora's box gets more and more volatile. Also, Diversity is not only necessary in cybersecurity because our digital landscape needs it, but it is a human right for this career path to be accessible to every professional regardless of demographic.

The fight for diversity in cybersecurity is not just about females; It is about all the people who feel like they would not belong, and who are being discouraged by societal standards; because each new mindset provides a different perspective, and each new perspective provides an innovative solution to make the cyber world a secure place for everyone.

*It is widely known that cyber security is still a very male dominated industry, even though it is 2024. Why do you think there are so few women in cyber security?*

"If you can hack in a hoodie, you can hack in a ballgown too." is something I said recently on a podcast episode.

Think about it: when was the last time you saw a relatable female hacker in a movie who wasn't portrayed as a lone wolf or devoid of "feminine" interests? As a teenager, I see part of the problem in the limited representation of female cybersecurity professionals in popular culture and media. In today's Digital world, our mindsets and ideals are heavily affected by the content we consume online.

My own experience reflects this. As a child, I loved expressing myself through fashion and makeup, but seeing mostly male hackers on screen made me subconsciously associate the field with someone I couldn't be. That's why characters like Alycia from "Salvation" being the female leader of a hacker group and Mel from "The Takeover" being an ethical hacker who loved painting her nails, were game-changers for me. They showed me that you can be passionate about technology while still being yourself.

This lack of diverse role models is just one reason young girls might hesitate to enter cybersecurity. It's why I started "HackWitHer," an initiative to shatter the perception of difficulty and empower girls to explore their cybersecurity potential.

The future of cybersecurity needs diverse perspectives and innovative solutions. We need to break down stereotypes and create a space where everyone feels welcome to contribute their unique talents. By supporting initiatives like "HackWitHer" and encouraging accurate portrayals in media, we can open doors for the next generation of cybersecurity professionals, whoever they choose to be.

*Who are your role models in cyber security?*

My one true female role model is my mom; She has shown me what a strong woman is like. She taught me the meaning of love and passion, pain and resilience and ethical values that I carry even in my cybersecurity career. As for her professional background, she has a Bachelor's in science, education and has her Master's in Computer Applications. She left her job to take care of me full time and she is the sole reason I am here today. Other than her, I've been so fortunate that If i were to name all my role models, This book would have at least a thousand pages. I am eternally grateful to all of them.

*If you could go back in time to your first days in the industry, what would you do differently or tell yourself?*

You know how it's said that If you can't change the world, change your neighbourhood?

After the launch of HackWitHer, I started posting videos explaining complex cybersecurity concepts using relatable analogies, concepts that i once struggled to understand. Recently, I received a DM saying that an 8 year old girl learned about the OSI Model just by listening to me explain it with the reference of a chocolate factory!

So If I could go back in time, I would spend a lot more energy giving back to the community that has welcomed me with more love than I could ever imagine, especially young women interested in cybersecurity. I would have created a blog or vlog documenting my journey, the challenges I faced, and the resources that helped me along the way. By sharing my learnings openly, I hope to inspire others and make their paths a little smoother.

In the future, I hope to mentor and create resources that help bridge the gap for aspiring professionals, particularly those from underrepresented groups. I believe that by sharing our knowledge and experiences, we can build a more inclusive and resilient cybersecurity community.

*And finally, tell us a few fun things about yourself! Do you have an unusual hobby for example, or a fun fact about yourself that you can share?*

I love to paint my nails(especially in glitter) because when they reflect off my laptop screen, they look like absolute magic! Also, I've been boxing for 3 years and I've been learning Muay Thai since December 2023. Another fun fact: If I weren't so head over heels for cybersecurity, I would be a Physicist.

# Sarah Knowles

**Job Title:** Co-Founder and CEO

**Company/Organisation:** Shift Key Cyber Ltd

*Tell us a bit about your background, your career to date and what you currently do in cyber security.*

I have been in IT and cyber security for over 30 years now, but my very first role was in HR for a local authority. After a few years, I transitioned into an IT Support role, moving into a private sector role for a managed service provider. I was able to progress into more senior roles as my skills developed and move into technical consulting roles. From there, I was able to pivot into areas focusing more on governance, risk and compliance aspects of cyber security, and two and a half years ago, I was fortunate to be in the position to co-found a female-led consultancy business.

No two days are the same, but typically I am working with customers to help improve their cyber resilience so that they are better protected from today's cyber threats and to help build their knowledge of how to best protect their business. I help companies gain certification to standards such as Cyber Essentials and ISO 27001, as well as complete audits. I am on the Technical Advisory Board for The Cyber Scheme, and an assessor for the Cyber Advisor scheme. I also teach and mentor newcomers into cyber security. And I was one of the first cohort to become a Chartered Cyber Security Professional registered by the UK Cyber Security Council.

*How did you get into the field of cyber security?*

I was working as an IT Manager for an insurance company, and the industry was becoming more regulated with more compliance requirements. As frequently occurs in IT, I was given the task of implementing the governance and compliance structure within the business. That was 20 years ago, and I haven't looked back!I was working as an IT Manager for an insurance company, and the industry was becoming more regulated with more compliance requirements. As frequently occurs in IT, I was given the task of implementing the governance and compliance structure within the business. That was 20 years ago, and I haven't looked back!

*What are the main challenges you've encountered as a woman in cyber security, and how did you overcome them?*

Certainly in the past there were challenges, especially when I was in technical roles. I was frequently the only woman in the team and as such I felt there was a pressure to show that I wasn't there to make the numbers up, but that I was just as good as everyone else. In fact, the only pressure here was the one I was placing on myself.

*What are the things you've learned being a woman in the cyber security industry?*

Be confident in your skills, and speak up. I remember being in a workshop, and a question was asked about how to proceed with a particular problem. I thought I had a solution, but it seemed so simple in my mind that I didn't speak up for fear of sounding foolish. After a period of time, one of the other guys volunteered a proposal which was identical to the one I had formed in my head. He was applauded for his ingenuity. From that day, if I have a thought on something, I now speak up regardless of who else is in the room.

*What advice would you give to women who would like to join the cyber security industry?*

Believe in your capability and know your opinion or perspective can add value. And more importantly, you belong. There are so many support networks now get involved, share your experiences and listen to experiences of others.

*What role does diversity play in cyber security?*

One of my favourite sayings is "the definition of insanity is doing the same thing over and over, and expecting a different result".

Diversity is crucial to every sector, not just cyber. We face different challenges every day, and we can't solve all of these doing it what has always been done in the past. We need fresh ways of thinking about these problems, and that can only be achieved by having a diverse workforce. It is essential that we have different perspectives on solving problems that are prevalent in today's organisations.

*It is widely known that cyber security is still a very male dominated industry, even though it is 2024. Why do you think there are so few women in cyber security?*

I think the problem is pipeline. If you want to have more women in cyber, it has to start in schools, and the encouragement that cyber is open to everyone. Now it is a while since I was at school, but girls were certainly discouraged from taking subjects such as computer science.

There are improvements now with programs such as CyberFirst and Girls Who Code. But these are still geared towards technical capability. Cyber is so much more than that. Yes, having technical knowledge is certainly beneficial, but being able to listen to a customer, explain risks, being able to audit, and fundamentally communicate are all key skills that are used in cyber.

*Who are your role models in cyber security?*

If I'm honest, I didn't really have any role models when coming into cyber. There wasn't anyone who I especially looked up to. But that said I have had some exceptional people who have guided and mentored me along the way. What is really important to me is that if I can change one person's view on cyber, and help to bring them into the industry then that surely has to be a step in the right direction.

*If you could go back in time to your first days in the industry, what would you do differently or tell yourself?*

I would be more confident in my own abilities and my belief that you can achieve anything you set your mind to.

Also Y2K will be a massive overhype!

*If you could give women considering a career in cyberse-curity one piece of advice, what would it be?*

Believe in yourself and don't be afraid to speak up. Trust your decisions. You absolutely have a role to play in cyber. Do not be in rush to find the perfect job, just be open to learning and the role that suits you will come along when the time is right.

*And finally, tell us a few fun things about yourself! Do you have an unusual hobby for example, or a fun fact about yourself that you can share?*

I used to be a competitive powerlifter, which involved picking up heavy things and putting them down again without breaking myself. I failed.

Nowadays, I'm a cat mum to a very demanding nine year old tuxedo kitty, and on a mission to look after and feed all the hedgehogs in the local neighbourhood.

# Amy Lewis

**Job Title:** Information Security Consultant

**Company/Organisation:** Risk Evolves

*Tell us a bit about your background, your career to date and what you currently do in cyber security.*

Going right the way back, I was never the best student at school, and I definitely attended more for the social aspect than for an education. I grew up in West London with just my mum and I, and we lived in an area that what was a little rough around the edges shall we say. I have always been a visual learner and my mum recognised the signs of dyslexia in me at a very early age. The borough that we lived in did not recognise the learning disability, so mum would often help me with little tips and tricks to help me remember spellings or letters etc. . . I still actually use these till this very day.

Managing people has always come pretty easy to me and I pride myself on being firm but very fair. After years of working in various management positions from pubs to a furniture shop, my personal life took a massive turn and I moved my then, two children to Edinburgh, leaving everything I owned behind. Once I had mentally put myself somewhat back together (divorce will do that) I decided to start my own cleaning company with a friend I had made when we moved. I was self-diagnosed as OCD back then, so being paid to clean seemed like the ideal situation to be in. 4 months later, COVID19 shut the world down.

I have always worked better under pressure, and I think I lived most my life in fight or flight mode until I was diagnosed with ADHD later in life (35y) The time during lockdown, I did what I have always done, 'what can I do to make this work for us?' I have always been the cup is half full not half empty kind of person. That is when I found the world of Governance, Risk and Compliance (GRC) and what doors it would open for the cleaning company. I knew commercial cleaning would definitely pay more and the boom in new builds being built in the Edinburgh area meant they were right on our doorstep. I started by finding out what requirements most of the big construction companies needed so we could be on their preferred supplier list, and I went from there. By the time the construction sites were allowed back open, we held a SMAS and CHAS accreditation with ISO9001 and ISO14001 on the horizon. I then banged down doors, well, email addresses and phone numbers until someone gave us a chance. Fast forward to 2022 and we had multiple construction sites and offices on our books. As much as I loved what we had built the stress of running your own business definitely lay heavy on me and the family life balance I really craved. So, in 2023 I decided to scale back the company to part time and pursue something I had really enjoyed in the early years of the setup, GRC.

*How did you get into the field of cyber security?*

Initially Cyber security scared the life out of me as I had always thought I was not technical enough to push a career in this field, but I had seen a re-training course that a few people I knew had completed and they were thriving even though they did not come from IT backgrounds. One was actually a nurse, and the other was a hairdresser. The course was with a company called CAPSLOCK and I had first seen them back in 2021. At the time I was far too busy with the cleaning company and I hadn't got to the stage I wasn't enjoying it yet (not that I would admit out loud anyway). In May 2023 I finally decided to apply and take that chance on myself. By that time, I now had 3 children and had remarried to a pretty incredible man who fully supported me in whatever I wanted to do as long as I was happy. The course was 4-month intensive full-time course, and it taught all the different aspects of cyber security. I absolutely loved it and their team-based learning and hands on approach was exactly what I needed to learn. I found I had so many transferable skills I had picked up over the years that I could use to build this new career.

*What are the main challenges you've encountered as a woman in cyber security, and how did you overcome them?*

As a woman with ADHD in cybersecurity, I've faced particular challenges needing smart solutions. One big hurdle has been staying focused and detailed in a field that demands precision. I do have a keen eye for detail and can often stop a mistake that many will miss, but juggling tasks and staying focused in the fast-paced cyber world has been tough. To tackle this, I've split tasks into smaller bits, used time management tools, and stuck to routines to cut out distractions. Also, talking openly with colleagues and asking for help and movement breaks when needed has been vital. For example, working with Risk Evolves has been amazing, the have a very strong flexible working policy that actually promotes flexible working and doesn't just exist to make the company look good. Being able to be honest and open about who I am and what I need has been the difference in me being able to do my job and not. Embracing my unique brain style and using it as a strength has helped me tackle problems creatively and stay strong in cybersecurity and compliance, despite the difficulties ADHD can bring. On the flip side I also can hyper focus on a task for 8-10 hours some days and often need to be reminded to take lunch on days like this.

*What are the things you've learned being a woman in the cyber security industry?*

Being a woman in the cybersecurity industry has taught me several valuable lessons. Firstly, I've learned the importance of resilience and perseverance in a male-dominated field. I first learnt this while constantly dealing with site managers in construction who 99% of the time were male. Facing stereotypes and biases can be challenging, but it's essential to remain confident in my abilities, stand my ground in a respectful way and continue pushing forward.

Secondly, I've realised the significance of building a supportive network of colleagues and mentors. Having people who understand, and support diversity and inclusion can make a significant difference in my day-to-day job. Additionally, I've learned the importance of continuous learning and staying updated on the latest trends and technologies in cybersecurity. The field is constantly changing, and staying informed is essential to remain competitive and effective in my role.

Lastly, being a woman in cybersecurity has highlighted the importance of representation and diversity in the industry. By actively promoting diversity and inclusion initiatives, we can create a more welcoming and fairer environment for everyone.

Overall, being a woman in cybersecurity has taught me resilience, the importance of community, the value of continuous learning, and the significance of diversity and inclusion. These lessons have not only shaped my career but have also enhanced my outlook on the industry as a whole.

*What advice would you give to women who would like to join the cyber security industry?*

My advice to women who want to join the cybersecurity industry is simple, go for it! Don't let any doubts or fears hold you back. Believe in yourself and your abilities. Take advantage of resources and support networks available to you, whether it's mentorship programs, online courses, or networking events. Be proactive in seeking out opportunities to learn and grow in the field, research is key. Remember that diversity is a strength, and your unique perspective and skills will bring value to the industry. At Risk Evolves, one of the key elements we use is peer reviews on work we have done, this is because two pairs of eyes are always going to better than one, and that goes from top management down to the ground. Lastly, stay resilient, stay curious, and don't be afraid to challenge the status quo. I think it's safe to say I definitely do not fit into the 'norm' and my managers and colleagues use that to their best advantage. The cybersecurity industry needs more women, so embrace the opportunity and make your mark! In the words of Shania Twain, let's go girls!

*What role does diversity play in cyber security?*

Diversity plays a crucial role in cybersecurity. Having a diverse team means bringing together people with different backgrounds, perspectives, and skills, (like a school muck around with late diagnosed ADHD) which leads to more effective problem-solving and innovation. In a field where we're constantly battling new threats and challenges, having diverse viewpoints can help us see things from all angles and come up with creative solutions. Additionally, diversity helps us better understand and serve the diverse range of users and stakeholders we aim to protect. It also promotes inclusivity and equality, making the industry more welcoming and accessible to everyone. Ultimately, diversity isn't just a buzzword in cybersecurity—it's a key ingredient for success. So, let's celebrate our differences and work together to make our digital world safer for all.

*It is widely known that cyber security is still a very male dominated industry, even though it is 2024. Why do you think there are so few women in cyber security?*

Despite progress in many areas, it's true that cybersecurity remains predominantly male-dominated, even in 2024. Several factors contribute to the underrepresentation of women in the field. Firstly, there's the issue of stereotypes and social expectations. From an early age, girls are often discouraged from pursuing careers in STEM fields, including cybersecurity. This lack of

encouragement and support can discourage women from considering cybersecurity as a possible career option.

Secondly, the existing gender imbalance in the industry can create a perception of isolation and lack of belonging for women who do enter the field. Without sufficient representation and support networks, it can be challenging for women to thrive and advance in their careers.

Also, there may be systemic barriers within organisations, such as unconscious bias in hiring and promotion practices, that effect the gender gap in cybersecurity.

Addressing these challenges requires a combined effort from all stakeholders. We need to challenge stereotypes, further inclusive cultures within organisations, and provide mentorship and support to women entering the field. By actively promoting diversity and inclusion, we can create a more equitable and vibrant cybersecurity industry that benefits from the full range of talents, knowledge and perspectives.

*Who are your role models in cyber security?*

In cybersecurity, I draw inspiration from several role models who have made significant contributions to the field. One of my role models is Dr. Sue Black, a renowned computer scientist and academic who has championed diversity in technology, including cybersecurity. Her work in raising awareness about the importance of women in STEM fields and her efforts to support women pursuing careers in cybersecurity are truly inspiring.

I also admire the work of Professor Mary Aiken, an expert in forensic cyberpsychology, who sheds light on the human aspects of cybersecurity and the intersection of technology and human behaviour. Her insights into the psychological factors behind cybercrime and cybersecurity vulnerabilities are invaluable.

Furthermore, I look up to individuals like Helen Barge, the MD at Risk Evolves, an entrepreneur and advocate for women in cybersecurity, who tirelessly pushes for diversity and inclusion in the industry, and my boss. Call me biased but she is a force to be reckoned with and an incredible leader. (I really want to say she is a badass but don't know if that acceptable)

These role models demonstrate dedication, expertise, and a commitment to making the cybersecurity field more inclusive and impactful. They serve as a source of motivation for me and many others in the cybersecurity community.

*If you could go back in time to your first days in the industry, what would you do differently or tell yourself?*

If I could turn back time to my early days in the industry, I'd tell myself one thing loud and clear: "Yes, you absolutely belong here." Imposter syndrome can be a real hurdle, especially in a field as dynamic and fast-paced as cybersecurity. I'd remind myself that my skills, knowledge, and perspective are valuable contributions to the industry, regardless of any doubts or insecurities. I'd encourage myself to embrace challenges as opportunities for growth, to be confident in my abilities, and to never shy away from asking questions or seeking support when needed. Most importantly, I'd reassure myself that I have what it takes to succeed in cybersecurity and that my presence in the industry is not only valid but also essential for driving positive change and innovation.

*If you could give women considering a career in cybersecurity one piece of advice, what would it be?*

Trust yourself and have a laugh along the way! Unfortunately, the world will always have people that will put you down or say you can't do it, but I am 100% behind you. Believe in yourself and your abilities. The cybersecurity industry may seem intimidating, especially with its male-dominated reputation, but don't let that frighten you. You have unique skills, perspectives, and strengths to offer, and the industry needs more diverse voices like yours. Embrace opportunities to learn and grow, be confident in your capabilities, and don't be afraid to carve out your own path. Seek out mentors and allies who can support and guide you along the way. Remember that you belong in cybersecurity just as much as anyone else, and your contributions can make a real difference in keeping our digital world safe and secure. So, go for it with confidence, and don't let anything hold you back!

*And finally, tell us a few fun things about yourself! Do you have an unusual hobby for example, or a fun fact about yourself that you can share?*

I would have to say I'm an unusual person all round, on the outside I am a major girly girl, but also love to live in a tracksuit if I can. I LOVE a fantasy novel, (thank god for Audio book, as dyslexia and reading do not go well together) usually about vampires, werewolves, or anything out of this world, I think it helps my mind escape from the everyday pressures of being a working mum and wife.

FUNFACT – When I was 11, I was the fastest girl in swimming in Hammersmith and Fulham borough, I could do a 25 metre length in 10.9 second.

# Jacqui Loustau

**Job Title:** Founder and Executive Director

**Company/Organisation:** Australian Women in Security Network (AWSN)

*Tell us a bit about your background, your career to date and what you currently do in cyber security.*

I started my early career working in a number of IT helpdesks, PC Support and as a UNIX administrator, while studying Information Systems. My parents encouraged me to touch type at a young age and I was always curious about computers and helping people by fixing their problems! While travelling in Europe, I had the opportunity to upskill from working in a helpdesk to retraining as a cyber security consultant.

I worked for various clients, across Europe, designing and implementing AV systems, PKI systems, IAM systems etc, doing Risk Assessments and technical assurance reviews. And I even got the wonderful opportunity to manage a helpdesk at one of the venues at the Greece Olympics. When I came back to Australia, I worked for several Australian companies, performing SOC2 audits on a SOC, fixing DLP systems, working on IAM, PAM solutions. This then took me to the cybercrime team within a big bank in Australia, and this was when I first saw the terrible effects of small businesses when they got hit by cyber criminals. I then worked for a small Australian start-up that helped small businesses with their cybersecurity, and I loved it. This helped set me up (and gave me the guts) to then go out on my own and start a not-for-profit association.

*How did you get into the field of cyber security?*

I was working in the IT helpdesk of a company in London, and had the opportunity to upskill with the organisation. They took the best engineers across the world (+ me) and trained us in networking, Microsoft, information security and project management. At the end of this intense training, they asked us if we preferred to go into networking or information security. I chose cyber!

*What are the main challenges you've encountered as a woman in cyber security, and how did you overcome them?*

Early in my cyber security career, I was fortunate to hardly feel discriminated against. A few times I've had people challenge me with the 'you only got that role because you are a woman', 'you can't do that role as they are looking for someone more technical', 'you shouldn't work in penetration testing as you are a good communicator and would get bored', 'you do not have the skills to do this job'. It's very easy to listen to these comments and not pursue something that you think is interesting and that you want to do. But I managed to just push through with the encouragement of trusted people around me.

*What are the things you've learned being a woman in the cyber security industry?*

Women bring diverse skills which are really needed for cyber security. In our relatively young industry (compared to other sectors), we need more innovative, creative, analytical, curious, intelligent, highly organised, multi-tasking, empathetic, personable people to help protect people, information, companies, and countries. Different brains bring different perspectives and innovation.

*What advice would you give to women who would like to join the cyber security industry?*

- Network – it's the best way to understand the types of jobs in the cyber security industry, to build strong connections and your future village (Tip: Do not ask them for a job!). Join your local industry associations and attend conferences.

- Get a mentor – to help guide you through different stages of your career. (Tip (Do not ask them for a job!)

- Practice/training/CTF's – to upskill and to demonstrate your competencies and passion. Try to do as much practice with the free training available and write papers/present on it.

These are the steps I usually go through with women who are trying to enter the field:

1. Know your passion and what motivates you. Do you like solving puzzles/mysteries/problems. Do you like helping people? Do you like connecting people?

2. Understand your strengths. Are you persistent and won't give up when a problem presents itself. Delivery-focused. Do you like researching and learning? Do Is it that you can see things before it happens?

3. Define your knowledge and skills. Can you be cool as a cucumber during pressure? Can you triage and logically think through problems? Can you influence and persuade people? Do you understand a particular industry's business processes and can see/understand risks?

4. Do the homework! Determine what type of cyber roles would suit your passion and strengths and could use your current knowledge and skills.

If you have the curiosity, drive, love of solving problems and helping people, you must persist!

*What role does diversity play in cyber security?*

It helps us to look at things differently. For example

- **Those from different cultures,** bring the knowledge and skills from their countries and other sectors. Those from different age groups, brings new perspectives and considerations that we can learn from the past and the learn about future/emerging technologies

- **Those from different neurodiverse minds,** bring different innovative ways of solving problems and seeing the bigger picture

- **Those from different industries and backgrounds who are changing to cyber,** bring years of experience that we need to learn from and apply to our industry

- **Those from different genders,** bring culture changes and interesting perspectives on challenges

*It is widely known that cyber security is still a very male dominated industry, even though it is 2024. Why do you think there are so few women in cyber security?*

In Australia, according to the RMIT-AWSN Gender Dimensions of the Cyber Security Sector, women in cyber security are only 17%. However, this has been slowly changing over the last decade. Although the ratio looks bleak, "from 2016 to 2021, women's numbers in ICT Security Specialist roles grew fourfold while men's grew threefold".

Some of the reasons why we have such low numbers of women in this sector are:

- **When we are trying to attract them:** It's mainly because of perception. There is a perception that cybersecurity is highly technical, hard and you will be hanging out with a bunch of blokes in a hoodie in the basement (not that there is anything wrong with hoodies in a basement).

We need to change this imagery and to get more women speaking about what they do and what an exciting sector this is to work in.

- **When we get them into studying cybersecurity:** The accessibility of good training (cost, time, place, ability to ask questions without judgement), is a barrier. Women sometimes leave when they don't feel like they belong.

  Ensure the women can connect with inclusive industry groups to keep them motivated.

- **When women are trying to get into their first job:** They are not applying for jobs (as the JD is too complex) or they don't get an interview (as they undersell themselves). The saying is true that when a woman doesn't tick all the boxes, they won't apply.

  Re-think the way you write the job description, asking for competencies, and aptitude, rather than 'expert' 'world-class' 'ninja' and asking for years of experience on a specific version of a technology. You can use language checkers and gender decoders to help with that.

- When women are working: They can have challenges in certain companies and teams who question their competencies, don't invest in their skills, and don't promote them to leadership positions.

  When you recognise a women with high potential. Ask them what they need in order to succeed and ask them if you are doing enough. You maybe surprised at what they will say.

*If you could go back in time to your first days in the industry, what would you do differently or tell yourself?*

I would tell myself that being the CEO/CISO/CSO or a people manager doesn't mean you are successful or have 'made it' or to make a difference. You can be an expert in your area, run your own business, or even teach, as long as you are passionate about it and you get out of bed every day loving what you do.

Don't be afraid to ask for help when you want it. This industry is very giving and generous with their time.

*If you could give women considering a career in cybersecurity one piece of advice, what would it be?*

Working in cybersecurity is the most awesome, rewarding career. You can do it anywhere in the world, you get to work with some of the brightest minds, you can make a difference and you could never get bored, as every day brings new challenges to solve. Persevere and go for it!

*And finally, tell us a few fun things about yourself! Do you have an unusual hobby for example, or a fun fact about yourself that you can share?*

I climbed the Mont Blanc!

# Emma Mackenzie

**Job Title:** Information Security Governance Analyst

**Company/Organisation:** abrdn

*Tell us a bit about your background, your career to date and what you currently do in cyber security.*

I was an award winning hairdresser and makeup artist, running my own business for 10 years but in 2022 I reskilled in Cyber Security and landed my first (and current) role as an InfoSec Governance Analyst. My role involves alot of due diligence questionnaires, third-party assurance reports, and mailbox queries aswell as creating reports in Power BI, compliance assessments and policy reviews and I love every minute of it.

*How did you get into the field of cyber security?*

A family friend had been encouraging my husband to change careers into the field and had recommended a bootcamp. I looked in to it, signed up for the precourse and was pretty much hooked fromt the get go. I completed all the pre course work in less than 2 weeks and then went on to do a couple of the free Cisco courses whilst I waited to start the 16 week full time bootcamp. Everyone kept telling me not to do too much or I'd end up getting board, I didn't. The bootcamp was pretty intensive, working with a small team on every problem and project which helped enhance our collaboration skills as well as building the knowledge we needed to graduate. I spent 16 weeks attending my online classes full time during the week, studying in the evenings and working in the salon at the weekends and still fitting in time with my husband and 3 kids. It was tiring but totally worth it as I graduated the course whilst also achieving my CISMP and a foundation certificate in ISO 27001.

*What are the main challenges you've encountered as a woman in cyber security, and how did you overcome them?*

Having only been in the industry since November 2022, I have been lucky enough not to have encountered any challenges as a woman. My team are 50% female and I have some amazing female role models within my immediate team and the wider company to look up to and an extremely encouraging and supportive male manager.

*What are the things you've learned being a woman in the cyber security industry?*

I have learned that not all woman have been as lucky as I have been. Cyber is still a very male dominated industry and we all need to be doing everything we can to encourage more women to get involved.

*What advice would you give to women who would like to join the cyber security industry?*

I'm a firm believer of 'anyone can work in Cyber, no matter what their background'. If you have a keen interest and a desire to continuously learn, then Cyber is a great Industry to work in. There are so many opportunities out there, you just need to be willing to put yourself out there.

*What role does diversity play in cyber security?*

Diversity plays a massive role in Cyber security and this needs to be encouraged more. If everyone comes from the same background, has the same education and essentially thinks the same, then how will we ever come up with new ideas. Diversifying the industry brings in fresh new perspectives and creative solutions.

*It is widely known that cyber security is still a very male dominated industry, even though it is 2024. Why do you think there are so few women in cyber security?*

I think its because we tend to 'do' what the people around us do, aiming for careers that we see as achievable because we have seen real women doing them such as working in childcare, teaching, office work etc. All the main stream roles that we have grown up with. If it hadn't been for my male friend having a career in Cyber then I would never have known it was an industry that I could thrive in.

*Who are your role models in cyber security?*

There are so many fantastic and inspirational women out there who are great role models but if I have to name just a few then I would say Jude McCorry, Jenny Radcliffe and Lisa Forte as well as the women I am lucky enough to work with because they are all pretty fantastic.

*If you could go back in time to your first days in the industry, what would you do differently or tell yourself?*

Still being quite new into the industry, I don't think I would do anything differently. I try to make the most of every opportunity I can and have achieved so much in my first year in Cyber.

*If you could give women considering a career in cybersecurity one piece of advice, what would it be?*

Learn as much as you can but there will always be something new around the corner to keep you interested and apply for the job even if you only meet a few of the requirements. What's the worst that can happen?

*And finally, tell us a few fun things about yourself! Do you have an unusual hobby for example, or a fun fact about yourself that you can share?*

One of my favourite things to do is hill walking wether it be the local Pentland Hills for the afternoon or setting off in the car at 4am to go climb a Munro. The journey to the summit could take in all of the seasons in the space of an hour, walking on rubble, climbing endless amounts of stairs and trudging through bog whilst trying to make it to the top in hopes of seeing that amazing view that is never promised. The walk back down again is equally as horrific but the sense of achievement I feel for finishing it is worth every ache, pain and blister. It is definitely good for the mind and soul.

# Jelena Z. Matone

**Job Title:**

**Company/Organisation:**

*Tell us a bit about your background, your career to date and what you currently do in cyber security.*

Throughout my career, I have cultivated a distinguished background in the field of cybersecurity, with a proven track record of achievements and leadership recognition. I have held various positions in prominent global organizations in Canada and now in Europe, allowing me to hone my skills and expertise in the industry.

I am privileged to hold the Senior Head CISO position at the European Investment Bank. I lead many initiatives in this role, develop and implement cybersecurity frameworks and regulations, and contribute to the bank's cyber strategy.

*How did you get into the field of cyber security?*

My fascination with technology and dynamics sparked my interest in cybersecurity. I began my career in IT audit and compliance roles, which gave me a comprehensive under-

standing of the intricate relationship between technology and security. As I witnessed the growing importance of cybersecurity, I realized that it was a field that required dedicated professionals, and I promptly transitioned into specialized roles.

I have consistently worked towards enhancing my skills through certifications, training programs, and hands-on experience to stay up-to-date with the latest developments in the field. The dynamic nature of cybersecurity, with its constantly evolving threats and defense mechanisms, has further fueled my commitment to the field. Cybersecurity plays a critical role in safeguarding organizations from the ever-increasing threats posed by cybercriminals, and I am proud to be a part of this noble endeavor.

*What are the main challenges you've encountered as a woman in cyber security, and how did you overcome them?*

As a woman working in the field of cybersecurity, I have encountered specific challenges that are related to gender bias and stereotypes. However, I have always believed in the power of resilience, self-confidence, networking, and continuous knowledge to overcome these challenges. I actively showcase my expertise by participating in industry events and conferences. In addition, I have become an advocate for diversity and inclusion, working to create a working environment that is fair and inclusive for all by setting up the Women Cyber Force Association and W4C Chapter in Luxembourg and being an inaugurating President and current Founding Board Member.

I have effectively overcome gender-related obstacles by consistently delivering results and challenging stereotypes through my leadership. While it can be difficult to navigate these issues, it is important to remain focused on your goals, believe in your abilities, and work hard to succeed. With that, the sky is the limit.

*What are the things you've learned being a woman in the cyber security industry?*

As a woman in the cybersecurity industry, I appreciate the significance of breaking down gender barriers and promoting diversity. The experience has taught me that having a team with diverse backgrounds and perspectives is essential for fostering creativity and innovation. Furthermore, navigating a male-dominated industry has reinforced the importance of having mentorship opportunities and support networks in place. By embracing these lessons, I have grown personally and professionally and positively impacted the organizations I've worked with.

*What advice would you give to women who would like to join the cyber security industry?*

For women who aspire to enter the cybersecurity industry, my advice is to focus on your passion and work hard towards achieving it. To do so, you should acquire relevant certifications that will help you stand out in the field. Seek mentorship from established professionals who can guide you and provide valuable insights into the industry. Participate in industry events and stay updated with the latest trends and developments.

At the same time, please don't shy away from challenges but embrace them as opportunities to learn and grow. Be resilient, persistent in your efforts, and a vocal advocate for your capabilities. Demonstrate your expertise by actively contributing to the field and sharing your knowledge with others.

By doing so, you'll not only pave the way for your success but also inspire positive change within the industry. You'll become a role model for other women who aspire to enter the cybersecurity industry and help create a more diverse and inclusive industry. So keep pushing forward, stay committed to your goals, and don't let anything hold you back!

*What role does diversity play in cyber security?*

Diversity is an essential aspect of achieving success in the field of cybersecurity. It plays a pivotal role in bringing a wide range of perspectives to the table, which in turn helps to foster creativity and critical thinking. In the cybersecurity industry, where dealing with complex and ever-changing threats is the norm, diversity is crucial in ensuring that teams have a well-rounded approach to problem-solving. It enables individuals to approach challenges from different angles and provides a more comprehensive understanding of the situation, ultimately leading to innovative and effective solutions. Additionally, having a diverse workforce enhances the adaptability of teams to evolving challenges, making them better equipped to handle new and emerging threats. By embracing diversity, the cybersecurity industry can create a more resilient and dynamic environment that is better equipped to address the complexities of the modern digital landscape.

*It is widely known that cyber security is still a very male dominated industry, even though it is 2024. Why do you think there are so few women in cyber security?*

The under-representation of women in cybersecurity is complex and can be attributed to various factors. One of the primary reasons is the historical gender biases and stereotypes that have existed in the field for decades. STEM fields, including cybersecurity, have traditionally been considered male-dominated, which has created significant barriers for women trying to enter the industry.

Additionally, there needs to be more visible role models for women in cybersecurity, which can discourage those interested in pursuing a career in the field. Women also face limited exposure to cybersecurity opportunities during their education, which can further widen the gender gap.

To address such issues, concerted efforts are needed from various stakeholders. Industry players can promote inclusivity and diversity by creating a welcoming and supportive work environment for women. Educational institutions can take steps to increase the number of cybersecurity opportunities available to female students and provide them with the necessary support to pursue a career in the field.

Policymakers can also play a significant role in addressing

the gender gap in cybersecurity by promoting policies that support gender equality, such as offering scholarships and grants to women interested in pursuing cybersecurity careers. It will take a collective effort from all stakeholders to create a more inclusive and diverse cybersecurity industry where women have equal opportunities to succeed.

*Who are your role models in cyber security?*

I am drawn to the stories of those who have come before me - the trailblazers and pioneers who have worked tirelessly to build and shape this industry into what it is today. There are a few of them, friends, I look up to and learn from.

They are my actual examples of what can be achieved through hard work, dedication, and a commitment to doing what's right. Their contributions to the cybersecurity community are immeasurable. I am honored to draw inspiration from such encounters and networks as I navigate this exciting and challenging field.

*If you could go back in time to your first days in the industry, what would you do differently or tell yourself?*

If I could revisit my early days in the industry, I would emphasize the importance of networking and building a support system. Early on, connecting with mentors and industry peers can provide valuable insights and guidance. Additionally, I would encourage myself to be unapologetically confident in my abilities.

*If you could give women considering a career in cybersecurity one piece of advice, what would it be?*

Believe in yourself, pursue your passion relentlessly, and

actively seek opportunities to learn and contribute. Embrace challenges as opportunities for growth, and don't hesitate to advocate for yourself. Stay curious, keep learning, and be open to new challenges. By forging your path with confidence and resilience, you not only contribute to closing the gender gap in cybersecurity but also pave the way for future generations of women in the field. Keep going, and inspire others to do the same!

# Abigail McAlpine

**Job Title:** Cyber Security Researcher and Academic Lecturer

**Company/Organisation:** University of Huddersfield and Sheffield Hallam University

*Tell us a bit about your background, your career to date and what you currently do in cyber security.*

My journey into cybersecurity has been quite unconventional, starting from a background in marketing management. My career began in small companies with limited marketing budgets, where I quickly learned the importance of leveraging SEO (search engine optimisation) and social media algorithms to maximise our reach and engagement.

One particularly intriguing aspect of my early marketing days was discovering how to "hack" engagement algorithms on platforms like Facebook. I developed a process that involved utilising multiple sock accounts to artificially inflate initial engagement stats. At that time, the level of initial engagement directly impacted how much the algorithm on Facebook pushed posts to more users, especially in specific geographic areas. This experience taught me invaluable lessons about the vulnerabilities inherent in digital platforms and the potential for manipulation. It sparked my interest in cybersecurity as I realised the broader implications of exploiting algorithmic weaknesses for nefarious purposes. Today, in my cybersecurity role, I draw upon this unique background to approach problems with a different perspective. I understand firsthand how digital systems can be manipulated and the importance of robust security measures to mitigate such risks.

*How did you get into the field of cyber security?*

While managing newsletters and social media administration, I became acutely aware of the vast amount of data collected about individuals through innocuous pings, often without their understanding or consent. This realisation sparked a fervent interest in data privacy, prompting extensive discussions with peers and colleagues. Leveraging my need for an undergraduate dissertation in Business Studies, I seized the opportunity to conduct research on users' understanding of clickwrap and browsewrap agreements. The findings from this research propelled me further into the realm of privacy, information security and Human-Computer Interaction research.

As a culmination of my academic pursuits, I recently completed a thesis examining the Personally Identifiable Information (PII) of minors posted by parents on social media. This comprehensive study encompasses several dimensions, including the PII data parents self-disclose (about themselves and their children) on social media platforms, the observed behaviour of parents on social media as perceived by the public, and an analysis of existing laws and regulations aimed at safeguarding children from the oversharing of their parents. I hope one day to work on publishing the work, but it is currently in examiner hands.

Through this research, I aim to shed light on the complexities surrounding online privacy, particularly concerning vulnerable populations such as minors. My work underscores the importance of robust regulatory frameworks and heightened awareness among parents and guardians to ensure the responsible handling of personal data in the digital age.

I also had the opportunity to work for the Centre of Excellence in Terrorism, Resilience, Intelligence and Organised Crime Research and worked on Horizon2020 crisis-related research with social media analysis and warning message generation systems for water-related crisis. I also supervise cyber security students through their undergraduate research projects at Sheffield Hallam. Additionally, I write technology/cyber security think pieces, training and book chapters and I'm perpetually learning how much I don't know about what I don't know. It's a wonderful predicament in cyber security that you do not have the power, time or energy to know everything there is to know. There's always going to be students who come along and teach you something and it is wonderful to empower people at the beginning of their journeys and see them excel.

*What are the main challenges you've encountered as a woman in cyber security, and how did you overcome them?*

As a woman in cybersecurity, I've encountered several challenges that have required resilience and proactive strategies to overcome. One of the primary challenges is the pervasive gender imbalance within the industry, this can sometimes result in fewer opportunities for women to advance and succeed inside an organisation. This lack of representation can lead to feelings of isolation and the perception of being undervalued or underestimated.

To navigate these challenges, I've actively sought out mentors and allies within the field who have provided guidance, support, and advocacy. I am honestly so blessed by some of the connections I have made especially with other women in the industry who build each other up and the advocates and allies who understand the fight alongside us. Building strong professional networks has been instrumental in expanding my opportunities and fostering a sense of belonging within the cybersecurity community.

Additionally, I've focused on continuously enhancing my skills and expertise through ongoing education, certifications, and participation in industry events and conferences. There are a lot of people who have opinions about what I should be or what I should know or what I should or should not be doing. I think everyone has a bit of imposter syndrome, but it can be particularly prevalent for women in male dominated industries. I didn't come from a technical background and people struggle to understand where someone like me fits in organisations like theirs.

Another challenge has been overcoming implicit biases and stereotypes that may affect perceptions of my abilities and suitability for certain roles or responsibilities. I went to a well-known conference a few years ago with some male colleagues and saw women at a vendors in red bikinis and heels handing out flyers. I don't blame the women for it,

but it did unfortunately set a very terrible precedent for
some of the men working at or visiting the venue. I think I
was asked 30+ times if I was in "marketing" with some sort
of inuendo. I also accidentally introduced my colleagues to
insight on how badly women can be treated in this industry. I'd often ask vendors questions just for them to
completely ignore me, direct their response to my male
colleagues or be told not to worry about it, or even asked
personal questions in response to my questions. I also did
a speaking event in another country discussing how cyber
stalking can be used to progress into actual stalking then
was promptly followed around the event for several days.

*What are the things you've learned being a woman in the
cyber security industry?*

Reflecting on my experiences as a woman in the cybersecurity industry, I've learned invaluable lessons that have
shaped my perspective and approach. While I have always
considered myself to be resilient, I've encountered challenges that have tested my strength in unexpected ways.
One of the most profound realisations has been the existence of gender biases and prejudices that can significantly
impact professional opportunities. I've faced unwarranted
scrutiny and hostility when applying for entry-level roles,
solely based on preconceived notions formed before I even
entered the room. These experiences were deeply disheartening and served as a stark reminder of the some of the
harsher realities of the industry. It also showed me that
there is so much room for change and growth. There are
jobs in this industry that don't exist yet because the men
at the top of the industry don't think the same way women
do, they often navigate the world in totally different ways,
that's exciting. That's something to look forward to.

*What advice would you give to women who would like to*

*join the cyber security industry?*

Navigating gender-hostile environments requires a level of strength and resilience that not everyone possesses. I've come to understand that it is not my responsibility to change the minds of those who are unwilling to see beyond their biases. Instead, I've learned to prioritise my own well-being and seek out environments where I feel supported and valued. I've become discerning in selecting potential employers, placing a strong emphasis on finding organisations that prioritize diversity and inclusion. While this approach may limit some opportunities, I refuse to serve as a token representative for gender dynamics in the workplace. It's important to acknowledge that I am not a leader in this regard, and that's okay. I draw strength from recognising my limitations and focusing on areas where I can make a meaningful impact. I hold immense admiration for the women who lead the charge for change in the industry, and I am committed to supporting their efforts in any way I can.

Being a woman in cybersecurity has been marked by challenges, but also by growth and self-discovery. I remain steadfast in my commitment to advocating for inclusivity and equity in the workplace, while also prioritising my own well-being and professional fulfilment. I've made my own opportunities and worked in and with organisations who support women in cybersecurity. There are so many of them out there. Don't waste your effort on organisations that show you they have stunted their own opportunity to grow.

*What role does diversity play in cyber security?*

Diversity plays a crucial role in cybersecurity for several reasons. Firstly, a diverse workforce brings a variety of perspectives, experiences, and approaches to problem-solving, which is essential in tackling the complex and evolving nature of cyber threats. Different backgrounds and viewpoints can lead to more innovative solutions and help anticipate and mitigate vulnerabilities that may be overlooked by a homogenous team. In cybersecurity, we're dealing with adversaries who constantly adapt and innovate. Having a diverse team ensures that we can approach challenges from multiple angles and anticipate a wider range of potential threats. It is also so important to understand the users of applications or platforms, people like me who were manipulating algorithms before they understood how it falls into exploiting a vulnerability of a kind.

Additionally, diversity fosters a culture of inclusivity and mutual respect, which is essential for effective collaboration and information sharing within the team and across organisations. In today's digital age, information is more accessible than ever, and younger generations seem to possess an innate proficiency in navigating the vast landscape of collecting online data. As someone who has

prided myself on my ability to gather information, I'm both terrified and amazed by the sheer skill and resourcefulness of teenage girls in uncovering personal information. It's a testament to the evolving nature of technology and the need for constant vigilance in safeguarding our digital identities. While it may be intimidating, it's also a reminder of the importance of staying informed and adapting to the ever-changing cybersecurity landscape. It is wonderful and terrifying.

*It is widely known that cyber security is still a very male dominated industry, even though it is 2024. Why do you think there are so few women in cyber security?*

The under-representation of women in cybersecurity is a
multifaceted issue that stems from various factors. Firstly,
there are significant barriers to entry, including technical
skill requirements and the existence of 'old boys clubs'
within the industry. Many entry-level positions in cybersecurity demand specific technical skill sets that may be perceived as daunting or inaccessible to women, particularly
those who haven't traditionally pursued STEM-related fields.
There so much advice that it is simply overwhelming, looking at entry-level job options is not any better when they
list certifications that require years of experience. Those
responsible for cyber security recruitment really needs to
take a step back and evaluate what entry-level even means.

One major challenge is the misconception of what consti-
tutes an entry-level role in cybersecurity. For instance, certifications like CISSP require 5 years of experience, making
them inappropriate for individuals just starting their careers. This creates a paradox where entry-level positions
demand advanced qualifications, leading to a mismatch between job requirements and applicant qualifications. Additionally, the high cost of entry-level certifications can be
prohibitive for many individuals, further exacerbating the
issue of accessibility and inclusivity. Research has consistently shown that women are less likely to apply for jobs
unless they meet all the listed criteria, whereas men are
more inclined to apply even if they only meet a portion
of the requirements, this has been well known for over a
decade. This disparity in application tendencies can further hinder women's entry into cybersecurity, especially
when organisations demand a laundry list of qualifications
and experience for entry-level positions. Addressing this
issue requires a shift in hiring practices and a greater emphasis on potential rather than strict adherence to qualifications and certifications organisations show little interest

in funding themselves.

To promote gender diversity and inclusivity, significant investments need to be made in training, apprenticeship, and internship programs that are accessible to everyone, regardless of socioeconomic background. There is an expectation that people interested in this industry should eat, sleep and breathe security, I think that is more than often a luxury for the privileged few. It excludes a life, a person with interests outside the industry. It's another way people turn into numbers and in the case of cyber security some of this is voluntarily self-enforced expectations on others. Organisations must also reevaluate their hiring practices to ensure they are inclusive and equitable, focusing on skills and potential rather than rigid qualifications. Additionally, there needs to be a concerted effort to dismantle existing barriers and biases within the industry, fostering a culture of inclusivity and support for all individuals interested in pursuing a career in cybersecurity. In some cases there is very little to suggest that organisations are willing to invest in their employees beyond a paycheck.

*Who are your role models in cyber security?*

I try to refrain from idolising individuals in the cybersecurity domain, as such pedestals may inadvertently impose undue pressure for perfection or perpetual pursuit of achievements which can

be harmful for individuals mental health. I draw inspiration from a diverse array of figures within the industry, valuing their contributions and insights.

Among those whom I admire is Melanie Oldham MBE,

the founder of Bob's Business[1], who played a pivotal role in the inception of the Yorkshire Cyber Security Cluster (YCSC)[2]. Additionally, I am inspired by the endeavours of CAPSLOCK[3] founders Dr Andrea Cullen and Lorna Armitage, whose initiatives adeptly introduce newcomers with foundational industry principles, fostering both knowledge and confidence. Having personally benefited from their bootcamp, I enthusiastically recommend it to those seeking a supportive entry point into the field.

I am humbled by the accomplishments of former peers who have excelled beyond my own capabilities. Reflecting on interactions from events such as the inaugural Glasgow Caledonian Cyber Convention (G3C), I am inspired by the growth and achievements of individuals whose diligence and passion have propelled them to success. Particularly noteworthy are the contributions of Security Queens[4] and individuals like Kinga Kieczkowska [5] and Hela Lucas [6], whose work continually pushes boundaries, educates and expands horizons within the cybersecurity landscape.

In the realm of academia, I recommend the work of academics such as Prof. Bill Buchanan OBE [7], whose insightful Medium blogs elucidate complex topics like encryption and applied cryptography. Additionally, the community-oriented efforts of Danny Dresner FCIIS who invests a lot of time into diverse educational initiatives, content creation, and interviews, exemplify a commitment to fostering knowledge exchange and advancement within the cyberse-

---

[1] https://www.bobsbusiness.co.uk
[2] https://ycsc.org.uk
[3] https://capslock.ac
[4] https://securityqueens.co.uk
[5] https://kieczkowska.wordpress.com
[6] https://helalucas.github.io
[7] https://billatnapier.medium.com

curity community.

*If you could go back in time to your first days in the industry, what would you do differently or tell yourself?*

I wish I had invested more time honing my technical skillsets and deepening my understanding of risk management principles at the beginning of my journey. While my journey has encompassed diverse experiences and achievements, I recognise the pivotal role that having some technical proficiency plays in navigating the complex landscape of cyber threats. It is not a necessary element of being a cyber security professional but I've found that learning more of these skills has helped me to understand their application in automation. Also one that people don't talk about enough is Microsoft Excel/Word skills, more advanced courses will help build up knowledge that you will use for a long time, I see a lot of students undervaluing those skills currently.

In hindsight, pursuing certifications focused on risk management would have fortified my expertise and equipped me with the frameworks necessary to effectively assess, prioritise, and address vulnerabilities within digital environments.

*If you could give women considering a career in cybersecurity one piece of advice, what would it be?*

I highly values the insights and advice of female peers in the field, I have found immense inspiration and guidance from the perspectives of other women navigating the cybersecurity landscape. Their experiences and expertise offer invaluable insights into the unique challenges and opportunities within our industry. The contributions of female cybersecurity professionals have been instrumental in shaping industry best practices and driving innovation.

From thought leadership in areas such as

threat intelligence and incident response to pioneering initiatives aimed at bridging the gender gap in cybersecurity, their impact is profound and far-reaching.

I advise following work by those who identify as neurodivergent or disability advocates, I have gained a deeper understanding of the importance of fostering inclusivity and diversity within our field. The content they have produced has empowered me to navigate professional challenges with confidence and resilience, while also advocating for greater representation and equity within the cybersecurity community for myself and others. Together, we are forging a path towards a more inclusive, resilient, and dynamic cybersecurity landscape.

*And finally, tell us a few fun things about yourself! Do you have an unusual hobby for example, or a fun fact about yourself that you can share?*

I used to volunteer in community and student radio stations. I have always been one of those people who consumes copious amounts of music, I can't really stand silence so I always had background music on. I listen a variety of different genres and found this to be a great way to destress during my FE and HE studies. While in university I ended up running the station and put on live events, socials, and gained investment into the studio from the local community, as well as creating the stations first 24 hour broadcast for charity. I've always been big on re-investing into the community that invests in you. This hobby not only allowed me to explore my passion for music but also honed my communication skills and ability to think on my feet – qualities that are certainly beneficial in the fast-paced world of cybersecurity. I've been considering where these skills fit alongside my profession now and I've got some ideas. For now I've curated a section of my website [8] called "Waste time with Me" for fun playlists under different themes and different cozy games, books and a curated list of ways to take a break.

---

[8]HiAbigail.co.uk

# Connie McIntosh

**Job Title:** Head of Security, Market Area

**Company/Organisation:** Ericsson Global

*Tell us a bit about your background, your career to date and what you currently do in cyber security.*

I have worked in Government Classified Networks, for the Government National Cyber Security Emergency Response team and as Head of Security for Ericsson Market Area I am responsible for Cyber Security, Information Security, IT Security, Operational Security in 45 Countries.

*How did you get into the field of cyber security?*

I studied at University of Canberra and then applied for a very nondescript role which ended up being a Classified Government Security role so I say that Cyber Security chose me. :) I absolutely have loved every minute of my career journey.

*What are the main challenges you've encountered as a woman in cyber security, and how did you overcome them?*

When I started there were absolutely no women in leadership roles in Security, it was 100% a mans world and fortunately for me I grew up with all brothers and didn't see myself as any different from the boys. So I never saw this as a barrier however there were a few bosses who thought women should be home in the kitchen not working and much less not working in Security and gave me a bit of a hard time but as i said I grew up with brothers and not much bothers me.

*What are the things you've learned being a woman in the cyber security industry?*

Be yourself. Don't try to be anyone else, don't try to fit into any stereotype that you are not. Authenticity, resilience, persistence and passion will take you as far as you want to go.

*What advice would you give to women who would like to join the cyber security industry?*

Just do it, try a few different areas of cyber security until you find the area that you resonate with.

*What role does diversity play in cyber security?*

The more diversity the better, I have really seen the benefits in my own teams where we have a good mix of diversity to get great outcomes. What it allows is a range of thinking and ideas that you lack if you have a less diverse team.

*It is widely known that cyber security is still a very male dominated industry, even though it is 2024. Why do you think there are so few women in cyber security?*

I think there is still a stigma amongst young women who believe that you need to be a coder to get into cyber, this couldn't be further from the truth, there are so many roles that do not require any coding and we need to educate schools to help convey this message.

*Who are your role models in cyber security?*

I have an amazing Chief Security Officer in Ericsson who is an amazing role model, who demonstrates the ability to bring everyone along the journey, a great strategic thinker who can see the bigger picture.

*If you could go back in time to your first days in the industry, what would you do differently or tell yourself?*

Speak up more in your early years, you have great ideas and be open to sharing.

*If you could give women considering a career in cybersecurity one piece of advice, what would it be?*

Find a role model or mentor, understand all of the exciting opportunities available across the field of Cyber.

*And finally, tell us a few fun things about yourself! Do you have an unusual hobby for example, or a fun fact about yourself that you can share?*

I am passionate about everything I do and whilst studying and working in cyber I was heavily invested into fitness and became a two time Australian Fitness Champion and a World Fitness Champion. Then I had two children and juggled working and keeping fit along with being a Mum and studying my Masters degree.

# Hazel McPherson

**Job Title:** Chief Information Security Officer

**Company/Organisation:** ALD Automotive

*Tell us a bit about your background, your career to date and what you currently do in cyber security.*

I currently work as a Chief Information Security Officer (CISO) in the UK for a financial services organisation owned by the French bank Société Générale. Previously I have worked in healthcare (NHS), local government, manufacturing, and distribution. My background has been mainly in Information Technology since 2001 but prior to that it can only be described as varied!

*How did you get into the field of cyber security?*

During my time with the NHS, I was aware of the need for security more so than ever when patient wellbeing was at the core of everything you do. Part of my professional development was to understand how cyber threats may impact the Trust and be in a position of knowledge on the subject to best advise members of the executive group. So, when an opportunity to be part of a pilot program with ISC2 came up via the Health & Social Care Information

Centre, I jumped at the chance. The program was looking into whether the HCISPP certification could be used to increase cyber security experience within the NHS. It was this experience that sparked by passion to learn more and started my journey to a full-time role in security.

*What are the main challenges you've encountered as a woman in cyber security, and how did you overcome them?*

The most obvious ones are being ignored at conferences and events in favour of my male colleagues and being addressed as 'guys' or 'gents' in a group situation. Others are a little less obvious but still difficult to deal with. Things like having to deal with indirect abuse, belittling, and mocking from technical colleagues. Being in a male dominated industry hasn't gone without sexually inappropriate comments from senior management either during my time in IT. Where it's been too bad, I have resigned and moved on. I don't want to work for an organisation who are happy with that kind of culture. Nowadays I a bit older and care less about speaking out so will challenge unacceptable behaviour directly, but you have to have a thick skin and belief in your abilities. Having a good team, and a network of peers to talk to is essential!

*What are the things you've learned being a woman in the cyber security industry?*

I've learned how to 'be more man'. And by that, I mean how to be heard in meetings, get my points across firmly, negotiate, and influence. Although I have seen change, we still live in a sexist world and sadly sometimes I have had to embrace that to get by. To be honest though, my experience in IT was far worse than my experience in cyber.

*What advice would you give to women who would like to join the cyber security industry?*

Do it for the right reasons. Getting into cyber without a true passion for it will damage your health. There is a lot of stress that goes with working in cyber, and that comes from multiple places most of the time. Burnout is very real, and you may not know it's coming. If you don't have a team of cyber people to talk to and support you where you are working, find one outside of the organisation because there are plenty of community groups – you are not alone!

*What role does diversity play in cyber security?*

Diversity in any industry is important but sadly there are still too many places where it doesn't happen. I think that diversity in cyber can challenge stereotypes and make workplaces more welcoming. For most of my 23 years in IT and Cyber, I have been the only woman on the team, so the single diverse voice is hardly ever heard. Nowadays my team is the most diverse I have worked with, and that wasn't deliberate for the statistics, when you get the culture right people want to be part of that.

*It is widely known that cyber security is still a very male
dominated industry, even though it is 2024. Why do you
think there are so few women in cyber security?*

Culture. Whether it's team, organisation, industry – the
responsibility sits everywhere. Too many conferences with
all male speakers, the language we use to address people being too masculine, positive discrimination leading to
imposter syndrome, lots of senior IT people are men and
cyber often reports to IT still, old school IT attitudes not
being inclusive, and controversially women not challenging
this.

*Who are your role models in cyber security?*

This is one I think about a lot, and I don't have an answer for. I admire lots of people for lots of reasons, I don't
specifically have role models. I think it's great that people do have role models and certainly I aspired to be like
people I admired in my younger years. These days I see
people with passion coming into the industry and making
positive waves, or being brave, and I admire them for that
and feel inspired by their energy.

*If you could go back in time to your first days in the in-
dustry, what would you do differently or tell yourself?*

This one is easy. Not everyone will share the same passion as you for cyber security! I came into the industry
absolutely overflowing with enthusiasm and passion, to be
very quickly disappointed by those outside of it. I would
tell myself to be measured, understand the business needs,
and address the security concerns important to where you
are – don't try and boil the ocean.

*If you could give women considering a career in cyberse-*

*curity one piece of advice, what would it be?*

Always be curious. Working in cyber is exciting and forever changing. You will need to change with it, frequently. Being curious will help you stay build relationships, continue learning, find new ways of doing things, and meet some great people.

*And finally, tell us a few fun things about yourself! Do you have an unusual hobby for example, or a fun fact about yourself that you can share?*

I'm currently halfway through a personal challenge to visit all the registered pleasure piers in the UK. When I started, I think I underplayed just how many there were!

# Elga Ximena Cardozo Moreno

**Job Title:** Cyber Security Engineer

**Company/Organisation:** IKEA

*Tell us a bit about your background, your career to date and what you currently do in cyber security.*

Fourteen years ago, I started my journey in cybersecurity, and along the way, I've worn many hats, including Senior Cybersecurity Engineer, Senior Cybersecurity Consultant, Privacy and Security Officer, IT Security Projects Engineer, and even Cybersecurity and Privacy Manager at PwC, my first one was information security analyst.

This adventure has taken me across continents, from South America to Europe, working in places like Colombia, Argentina, Panama, Peru, El Salvador, Brazil, and over to Sweden. I have gotten the chance to work across a variety of business types, from retail, financial services, tech industry, critical infrastructure, pure cloud startups, and doing consulting work. This has given me a pretty broad view of different industries.

Now, my focus is on building secure digital environments, paying special attention to governance, risk management, compliance, and cloud security.

*How did you get into the field of cyber security?*

My entry point into cybersecurity was serendipitous, after finishing my degree in electronic engineering, I was looking for a specialization course in IT networks. But the only thing available that was even close was this Information Security course. **So, I thought, "Why not?" and I went for it.** That choice was really an "aha" moment for me, mixing my skills in IT networks with my eagerness to always be learning, and quiet right away, I found myself completely absorbed in the cybersecurity field.

**Shifting into cybersecurity at a senior level and starting again as an analyst was tough, no doubt about it.** It felt like taking a few steps back at first. But looking back now, every bit of that challenge was worth it. It gave me a fresh start and a chance to really dive deep into the nitty-gritty of cybersecurity from the ground up

*What are the main challenges you've encountered as a woman in cyber security, and how did you overcome them?*

I'll never forget how it felt on my first day at university.

**Picture this: just five of us women in a lecture hall with about 500 guys.** Coming from an all-girls school, I was totally thrown in the deep end - no one warned me it would be like this. **It was tough proving my competence and that I belonged there**, but I leaned into what I do best: talking to people, understanding them, and yeah, getting the tech stuff done too - after asking many questions and put a lot of hands-on effort.

On my way through university, **some teachers hinted maybe I should try something else**, thinking my endless questions were a bit much. But then, there were those who really got behind me, pushing me to dig deeper and ask even more. For the ones who weren't sure about me, I proved them wrong by sticking with it and making it. And **for the ones who always had my back, I'm forever thankful**. Their support has been priceless, helping me **turn curiosity into my biggest strength**.

You know how it felt being one of the very few women in a class or a work meeting, like you stick out? I kept expecting the same thing when I started working, and it happened. But, honestly, working in Sweden it's been a nice surprise. Things here are way more balanced than I thought they'd be. It's pretty cool how I don't feel that much of a difference here, which lets me just get on with my work and show what I can do.

*What are the things you've learned being a woman in the cyber security industry?*

In all this time working in cybersecurity, I've learned a lot, especially about teamwork and this isn't about gender at all. Teamwork is super important because there is so much to know in this field, like understanding all the tech stuff, keeping up with the latest threats, and making sure everything aligns with the business side of things. Honestly, it is pretty much impossible for one person to know it all. That is why working with a group of people who focus on different things is key. Sharing what we know and learning from each other makes us all better at protecting against cyber threats.

*What advice would you give to women who would like to join the cyber security industry?*

I'd emphasize the **power of resilience and self-confidence**. Understand that the challenges you will face, from gender biases to proving your worth in a male-dominated field, are not reflections of your capability but opportunities to strengthen your resolve and leadership skills. Embrace your unique perspective and voice; they are crucial for innovation in cybersecurity. Seek allies and mentors, engage in communities that uplift women, and **never underestimate the impact you can make**.

*What role does diversity play in cyber security?*

Starting out in cybersecurity, **I quickly realise how crucial it is to see things from different angles and perspectives that only diversity bring to the table**, especially after a surprising turn of events. We were struggling to get the budget for a much-needed firewall upgrade, this request was overlooked, and then, out of the blue, money was found for employee bracelets -not even clients- by another department. That moment was a real wake-up call for me. This incident didn't just highlight the importance of aligning tech needs with business goals; it reinforced my belief in the strength of diversity. Being one of the few women in the field, it's been clear to me that bringing a variety of backgrounds and insights to the table is not just beneficial—it's essential for innovative solutions and truly safeguarding our digital spaces.

*It is widely known that cyber security is still a very male dominated industry, even though it is 2024. Why do you think there are so few women in cyber security?*

The gender gap in cybersecurity stems from societal biases and the lack of encouragement for women to pursue STEM fields. Changing this narrative involves not only promoting STEM education for girls from a young age but also creating supportive communities that empower women throughout their careers and in workplaces.

*Who are your role models in cyber security?*

My current rockstar is Cassie Crossley, author of the book "Software Supply Chain Security", but rather than pinpointing specific individuals, I draw inspiration from the collective resilience and achievements of women in STEM. Realizing that no one is perfect, I've learned to admire the positive qualities in those around me, striving to embody the best aspects of various role models, including the pioneering spirit of tech leaders and the supportive nature of community members.

*If you could go back in time to your first days in the industry, what would you do differently or tell yourself?*

To my younger self, I would emphasize the importance of perseverance and the value of making mistakes. Mistakes are not failures but opportunities to learn and grow. **The journey in cybersecurity is as much about personal development as it is about professional technical expertise.**

*If you could give women considering a career in cyberse-*

*curity one piece of advice, what would it be?*

**Embrace continuous learning and adaptability**. Staying informed and flexible not only enhances your skills but also prepares you to tackle new challenges confidently. This mindset is crucial in navigating the dynamic landscape of cybersecurity and establishing a successful career.

*And finally, tell us a few fun things about yourself! Do you have an unusual hobby for example, or a fun fact about yourself that you can share?*

A highlight of this journey has been my last year commitment to empowering girls and young women in STEM with #WESTEM . I've strived to inspire and encourage the next generation to explore their interests in these fields. This commitment extended to a new, enriching role last year, where I began volunteering to teach cloud cybersecurity classes with #REDISchool.

These volunteer sessions, focused on cybersecurity on cloud education, sharing knowledge and experiences in a field I am deeply passionate about. Teaching in English, my second language, added another layer of accomplishment and connection, bridging language barriers and fostering an inclusive learning environment.

# Sarah Norman-Clarke

**Job Title:** Director of Information Security

**Company/Organisation:** Houses of Parliament

*Tell us a bit about your background, your career to date and what you currently do in cyber security.*

I did a degree in History and then a Masters in Archives and Records Management and worked in the archive and records management field for over a decade. My career encompassed both Civil Service and the private sector having held a series of increasingly senior roles at in both the Civil Service and the private sector. Some career highlights include working at the MHRA during the period they were licensing the Covid Vaccines and my previous role as Head of Information and Cyber Security at the Department for Transport.

I have MA in Archives and Records Management, a BA in History and CISSP.

My current role is Director of Information Security at the Houses of Parliament which I have been doing for just over 1 year where I Provide senior leadership and oversight of effective information security risk management for both houses.

*How did you get into the field of cyber security?*

By accident. I started off in KIM then got involved in accrediting systems, then got a role which headed up both Cyber and KIM and found I quite enjoyed the cyber bits. I think it helps coming from a non-tech background.

*What are the main challenges you've encountered as a woman in cyber security, and how did you overcome them?*

I think the main challenge has been making sure my voice is heard, and also wondering if I've been invited to attend conferences etc solely because of my gender. I am lucky though as I have held quite Senior roles I haven't had too many challenges.

*What are the things you've learned being a woman in the cyber security industry?*

You have to believe that you have the right to be in the room.

*What advice would you give to women who would like to join the cyber security industry?*

Give it a go! And make sure you choose your organisation carefully to somewhere that has women in tech roles and at senior level.

*What role does diversity play in cyber security?*

A huge one. If we have diversity, we have different perspectives on how to do things, the impact of our decisions and new approaches. I don't think cyber security can evolve as a function without increasing our diversity.

*It is widely known that cyber security is still a very male dominated industry, even though it is 2024. Why do you think there are so few women in cyber security?*

I think there are a few reasons:

1. It's partly because schools don't highlight it as a career to female pupils,

2. There is research showing generally that women only apply for jobs for which they meet 100% of advertised criteria. We need to be bolder!

3. Lack of diversity in terms of speakers- if you see cyber speakers on TV they are normally men.

*Who are your role models in cyber security?*

Umm. I think Sarah Armstrong-Smith from Microsoft- it's not easy being so visible and working for somewhere so high profile. Plus she really tries to encourage women into the profession.

*If you could go back in time to your first days in the industry, what would you do differently or tell yourself?*

Not try to do everything. Accept what I don't know and that it's ok to ask others for advice.

*If you could give women considering a career in cybersecurity one piece of advice, what would it be?*

You will need resilience and a support network as it can be challenging and frustrating.

# Dr Ifeoma E. Nwafor

**Job Title and Organisations:** Principal Partner, IEN Legal Associates. Founder, Cybercare and Girls' Aid Foundation and CyberSecPolicy Girls Initiative. Co-Founder/Chief Product Officer, Decybr Inc.

*Tell us a bit about your background, your career to date and what you currently do in cyber security.*

I began my professional career in 2006 after being called to the Nigerian Bar as an advocate and solicitor of the Supreme Court of Nigeria. I started my legal practice journey as an Associate with Ajogwu & Ajogwu, SAN law firm. In 2017, I established IEN Legal Associates[1], a legal, research, and advisory law firm specializing in cybersecurity

---

[1] www.ienlegalassociates.com.ng

law, AI policy, gender, and women development.

I joined the academic world in 2018 and currently serve as a senior lecturer at the Faculty of Law, Godfrey Okoye University, Nigeria. My academic pursuit led me to earn a PhD in International Criminal Law, with a specialization in Cyber Law, in 2019 from the University of Nigeria. Additionally, I have the honor of being a European Union Erasmus+ Scholar at the Faculty of Business, Economics, and Law, TH Köln, Germany, as of 2022. My contributions to academia include developing the curricula and teaching content for the cyber law course at my institution. I was also a visiting scholar/researcher at the Faculty of Law and Criminology, Katholieke Universiteit, KU Leuven, Belgium, from November to December 2023.

My book, "Cybercrime and the Law: Issues and Developments in Nigeria," has received wide acceptance both within and outside Nigeria, and is now the recommended textbook for master's degree students in eight prestigious universities in Nigeria. The advance book review was published in the International Cybersecurity Law Review[2].

Driven by a passion for creating a safer cyber ecosystem and advocating for increased participation of women in combating cybercrime, I founded the CyberSecPolicy Girls Initiative[3] in March 2023. This initiative, part of the Cybercare and Girls' Aid Foundation, strives to close the gender gap in cybersecurity by providing free training and mentorship programs to girls and women interested in the cyber and technology fields. The initiative proudly boasts fifty registered members. I am also the Co-founder and Chief Product Officer of Decybr Inc.[4], a technology plat-

---

[2]https://link.springer.com/article/10.1365/s43439-023-00080-3
[3]https://cybersecpolicygirls.org.ng/
[4]https://decybr.com/

form that offers an extensive database of national and international legal resources on cybercrime and technology law.

*How did you get into the field of cyber security?*

I got into cybersecurity law and policy because of my passion for a safer ecosystem and the need for effective laws to mitigate the prevalence of cybercrimes globally.

*What are the main challenges you've encountered as a woman in cyber security, and how did you overcome them?*

In a male-dominated field, I faced challenges such as stereotyping and a lack of mentors/ mentorship opportunities. I decided to step in and change the narrative. The lack of mentorship opportunities led to establishment of the CyberSecPolicy Girl's Initiative.

*What are the things you've learned being a woman in the cyber security industry?*

I have learnt that "one woman can make a difference, a team of women working together can change the world"- Ifeoma E. Nwafor

Women are doers; we bring positive impacts in the cyber field, which is why we need to close the gender gap in the industry to achieve a safer cyber ecosystem.

*What advice would you give to women who would like to join the cyber security industry?*

Women comprise about 25

I would advise women interested in joining the industry

to reached out to experienced women professionals in the field for guidance, career path advice and mentorship/skill development opportunities.

*What role does diversity play in cyber security?*

Diversity and inclusivity play a crucial role in the cybersecurity field and all sectors of life. Fostering diversity in the field yield better results due to diverse opinions, techniques and innovation for a more diverse, inclusive and safer cyber landscape.

*It is widely known that cyber security is still a very male dominated industry, even though it is 2024. Why do you think there are so few women in cyber security?*

Stereotypes, bias and inadequate mentorship opportunities. Particularly in Africa, there are not enough networking events, online forums and mentorship programmes to connect women cybersecurity beginners and experienced professionals in the cyber field. These beginners need encouragement to navigate obstacles, build resilience and stay motivated in the pursuit of their cybersecurity careers.

*Who are your role models in cyber security?*

Professor Peggy Valcke and Carmen Corbin in the cyber security law space.

*If you could go back in time to your first days in the industry, what would you do differently or tell yourself?*

I don't think there is much I would have done differently.

*If you could give women considering a career in cyberse-*

*curity one piece of advice, what would it be?*

Go for it! There is plenty room for many more women in the cybersecurity industry.

# Dooshima Dapo-Oyewole

**Job Title:** Program Manager: Digital Transformation, Digital Skills, and Digital Trust

**Company/Organisation:** Confidential (Cyber Security GRC and Qualified Security Assessor Management Consulting Firm)

*Tell us a bit about your background, your career to date and what you currently do in cyber security.*

My career began as a broadcast radio journalist! After a decade of producing, presenting and training talent I transitioned into working at the world's 7th largest insurance group. During my time there I was exposed to the world of digital transformation and IT Risk Management when the EU GDPR privacy and security legislation came into place. To ensure compliance with the laws numerous changes were made to the enterprise architecture which sparked my curiosity. I found a mentor and coach in my big sister's best friend who encouraged and guided me to further explore the field and the rest is history. I currently work to enable enterprises leverage suitable, adequate and effective digital capabilities required to stabilise, optimise and improve their business operations as drivers of value creation,strategic competitiveness and risk/resource optimisation.

*How did you get into the field of cyber security?*

My mentor Julia Adoo Ishoribo PMP, CISA, CRISC, CFE literally told me this is the field I think you should explore and I took a chance on her intuition.

*What are the main challenges you've encountered as a woman in cyber security, and how did you overcome them?*

Information overload! Cybersecurity best practices and frameworks often involve complex and technical language, making it difficult for beginners to grasp. As a result, when women start out they may feel overwhelmed and need help understanding and processing this information.

What helped me to filter the "noise" is using tools like the Cyber Career Framework to identify what aspect of cyber I was interested in so I could focus my research and information consumption in that area. Also joining industry groups like ISACA and making use of their career development resources were extremely helpful.

*What are the things you've learned being a woman in the cyber security industry?*

You will burnout and struggle without community. Find a professional tribe and actively participate and contribute as you navigate the highs and lows of building a career.

*What advice would you give to women who would like to join the cyber security industry?*

There is endless opportunity in the field... believe in yourself and go for it! Take charge of your career

development by seeking out training and certification opportunities, as well as actively seeking out leadership positions where you can make a difference and serve as a role model for other women in the field.

*What role does diversity play in cyber security?*

Diversity is crucial to ensuring safety and security in our connected world. Threat actors do not discriminate, so sustainable solutions should come from diverse perspectives and experiences.

*It is widely known that cyber security is still a very male dominated industry, even though it is 2024. Why do you think there are so few women in cyber security?*

I think generally potential cybersecurity practitioners have a poor understanding of what cybersecurity is and what career path's are available. This leads to low exploration of the field. Additionally lack of relatable role models, mentors and sponsors to inspire action stop women from exploring the field. Finally we need to see more end-user education and cybersecurity awareness programs to close the gender gap in the industry. The more knowledge parents, educators and students have the more diverse groups including women will be encouraged to come into cybersecurity.

*Who are your role models in cyber security?*

I am inspired by many amazing professionals in cybersecurity both male and female. I admire the work and career path of individual's like :

- Juliet Okafor - Founder of Revolution Cyber

- Phil Retinger - CEO of Global Cyber Alliance

- Jamila Akaaga Ade - Head of the Cybercrime Unit at Nigeria's Ministry of Justice

- Dr. Regine Grienberger - Cyber Ambassador, Federal Foreign Office of Germany

*If you could go back in time to your first days in the industry, what would you do differently or tell yourself?*

I really would not do anything differently. . . all the mistakes and missteps were part of my learning journey, I would not want to glow up without growing up! I would say well done girl..keep going many surprises await.

*If you could give women considering a career in cybersecurity one piece of advice, what would it be?*

That doubt or fear you feel is false evidence appearing real..you really can do this! Take strategic steps to increase your competence and confidence.

*And finally, tell us a few fun things about yourself! Do you have an unusual hobby for example, or a fun fact about yourself that you can share?*

You will always find me brewing a cup of tea!I am an aspiring tea sommelier and I document different teas I've had around the world and share cybersecurity tips under the hashtag #CybersecuriTEAwithDoosh.

# Stephanie Lynch-Ozanar

**Job Title:** Information Security Awareness & Education Specialist/Employment Support Coach (Neurodiversity Skills Focus)

**Company/Organisation:** Co-op/Think Musique

*Tell us a bit about your background, your career to date and what you currently do in cyber security.*

After proving to be a bit of a science whiz at school and college, I embarked on the 'wrong' journey at university. I studied Biomedical Science at The University of Sheffield with the naive view that I would cure cancer or something just as spectacular. I found the advice given to me by career advisors and generally my lack of awareness about the world of work, I found I was stuck in labs and hated it. Shy and as quiet as I was, I realised I needed to be around people, not head down focusing on an experiment. I suffered from chronic anxiety whilst studying and so this encouraged me to think about a career supporting others with mental health challenges.

First job out of University, I worked for Rethink Mental Illness as a Recovery Worker. This involved supporting people in mental health crisis, often talking them out of suicidal situations, and offering emotional support and advice to carers. I think this is when I realised I was good at communications and relationships. The feedback I got from people using the services was positive, and this gave me the awareness that I liked to nurture and empower others.

Sadly, the area management at the time didn't do a great job of running the services and so after 3 years I decided to start a fresh. I followed the inner eco warrior in me and started working in Manchester's sustainability sector. This both involved Volunteer Management, Community Engagement, and Activism...also dressing up as a giant bee very often whilst sowing wildflower seeds with children. This led to me getting a job in communications at Manchester Climate Change Agency. My role was to translate complex information about sustainability from some of the biggest companies in the city and translate them into content for the masses. Here I learnt stakeholder management and how to create content. I also became a director for a food waste not-for-profit for a spell.

Wanting a career change yet again, I studied marketing

in my free time and then searched for my first marketing role. I don't remember every sending a LinkedIn CV, but I found one day I had an interview for the Cyber Resilience Centre for Greater Manchester (now North West) which is a police initiative to support SMEs. I got the role because of my not-for-profit background and stakeholder management experience. The very first day, I have a huge panic attack in the bathroom as imposter syndrome hit. This new field excited me, but I felt like a fraud. I had a brilliant project manager who was new to the field herself but really believed in me.

As my career in Cyber Security progressed, I studied a course in Governance, Risk and Compliance whilst working as a Marketing Campaign Manager at NCC Group. Once qualified, I worked in their compliance team as an internal auditor. I brought some new skills to the team including content design, but what really shone was my ability to help people feel comfortable when being audited. This meant I got the very best out of them.

When I saw a job come up at the Co-op for Education and Awareness Specialist, I threw my hat into the ring. It turns out, all my marketing and people skills learnt from other roles outside of cyber security were the perfect combo. Now I design e-learning and business wide communications campaigns. It is a wonderful mix of data and design, and I absolutely love it.

Going back to imposter syndrome...I had coaching for a year to help me beat it. Last year, this coach approached me to become a coach myself. She had a late diagnosis of autism which changed her life, she finally understood her place in the world. She set up a business to support people in the workplace who are neurodivergent. This includes helping them with Access to Work applications, 1:1

coaching with a focus on their employment skills and challenges, and co-coaching employers to help them create environments their neurodivergent employees can thrive in. She asked me if I would like to train up as she liked my people's skills and I jumped at the chance!

And that is me up to date, proof squiggly careers can work.

*What are the main challenges you've encountered as a woman in cyber security, and how did you overcome them?*

I have mentioned I suffered from imposter syndrome which is a mixture of not always having the most secure foundations growing up and also being an introverted person in an extrovert's world. This isn't directly related to cyber security, but coming into it, I felt like everyone would be clever except for me. I didn't see my worth.

Another challenge is pay, I have undervalued my worth a lot and it is only this year I am beginning to change this. Again, this probably down to being an introvert who has experienced anxiety and imposter syndrome, but I have noticed men progress quickly as they are less doubtful of their abilities.

One very recent challenge is having the presence of a man. I was on a panel, and I had someone feedback that I was relaxed and confident, but the difference in body language for the male panelists was more like they deserved to be there, whereas I was placing myself there. This was a powerful reflection and piece of feedback.

I think there are fewer women in this sector because it isn't encouraged enough at a school level, I think it was traditionally a male sort of industry and often girls and younger women didn't see themselves doing well. I hope this is changing from this level because I would

love to see more women in consultant/technical roles in the future. I like how non-technical skills are being valued more and it is allowing people from various career backgrounds like myself to enter the sector.

*What are the things you've learned being a woman in the cyber security industry?*

That the sector needs us! I was in an all-male team when in compliance at NCC Group but I was well respected and valued. In fact, they absorbed the skills I brought to the table. This team I feel was not the norm though, I was lucky to have such colleagues.

The women I have met across all fields have been nothing but brilliant in their own awesome way. I cannot imagine the sector without them, so it is an unsettling thought that were was once even fewer women than there are now.

*What advice would you give to women who would like to join the cyber security industry?*

This would be to be yourselves, don't undervalue your skills even if they don't seem as worthy as other colleagues because likely they are. I always like to keep learning, but also to remember not to over push yourselves. Take it steady and win that race in your own time, not because you must prove yourself.

*What role does diversity play in cyber security?*

It can be crazy in 2024 people need to explain this to think this but the role is that it is vital for any workforce. I think it is great that neurodiversity often gets a slot at security conferences, but I want to see the conversation move away from 'let's hire ND candidates' to 'how do we create an environment for colleagues to thrive, including ND colleagues. This is why I became a coach, as I want to help people grow in their roles. Diversity should never be viewed as 'them and us', I am hoping in my career span I see this change.

*Who are your role models in cyber security?*

It is really hard to answer! I respect and value so many people in this field. I think anyone who champions diversity are just fantastic, they are really changing the playing field.

I also love organisation like Capslock who support people from a number of angles to enter the sector. Again, changing the playing field and making things happen.

Oh also, the good people at The Cyber Helpline who work so hard to help the public experiencing some awful situations at the hands of hackers and cyber bullies/stalkers.

*If you could go back in time to your first days in the industry, what would you do differently or tell yourself?*

Steph, you are going to ace this!!! If I would have told myself whilst having a panic attack in the ladies toilets that I was going to work for a huge retailer talking to people about security I wouldn't have believed it. Neither would I have believed I would work for a

leading cyber security company auditing offices in Europe, or that I would sit on panels like Teiss and PrivSec discussing the latest security topics. I would tell myself the sky is the limit, and hand over the jet pack.

*And finally, tell us a few fun things about yourself! Do you have an unusual hobby for example, or a fun fact about yourself that you can share?*

Alongside my day jobs, I used to be a professional belly-dancer. I travelled the world dancing on cruise ships and Arabic weddings, parties etc. I retired before starting security, but it was 11 years of adventures and fun.

# Valerie Perlowitz

**Job Title:** CEO/Founding Partner

**Company/Organisation:** International Holding Company
LLC

*Tell us a bit about your background, your career to date
and what you currently do in cyber security.*

I am a serial entrepreneur with degrees in electrical, computer and cybersecurity engineering, and a management
degree. I started my career while I was in college working
for defense contractors and the Fortune 100. I worked with
computer networks and debugging software on the B1B
Bomber and Sikorsky's helicopters. I then became a consultant for Fortune 50 companies designing, implementing,
and maintaining large scale communication systems such
as MCI and the U.S. Federal Government telecommuni-
cation systems. I grew through the ranks from a tech-

nical contributor to a technical manager and eventually started my own businesses. As the President/CEO/Chair of the Board, I started, grew, and successfully exited product and services businesses serving the Global 1000, state and local governments, and the U.S. Federal Government, including the defense and intelligence communities. Part of the offerings were systems integration, network design, MSP/MSSP, cybersecurity, risk management, and outsourced services. I sold my last services business to a Special Purpose Acquisition Company (SPAC) which focused on agile software development, network management, cybersecurity, and program management for the recruitment, law enforcement, defense, intelligence, and commercial sectors. As a Board of Director member in charge of Strategy and IT as well as a Senior Vice President I was involved in the operations of the organization including Corporate Development, M&A, and divestitures. For an investment banking firm focused on the sixteen critical infrastructures, I was a Partner and the Chief Strategy and Corporate Development Officer and raised venture capital dollars for the commercialization of new cybersecurity and AI technologies from the national laboratories and universities. As we acquired a skills management and recruiting platform, I raised private equity to fund the growth of the company by organic growth and acquisitions. Currently as CEO/Founding Partner, I support companies in the areas of cybersecurity, AI, and quantum with risk management, framework design, business continuity, remediation, identity management, governance, policy, and compliance (GRC), and other business consulting services. I am still involved in fundraising for startups, growing companies, and large organizations, especially those building cybersecurity and AI platforms. I am a speaker and writer on business and technology subjects including starting, growing, and exiting businesses to policy, governance, and compliance in cybersecurity and AI.

*How did you get into the field of cyber security?*

During high school I went through a pre-engineering program that excited my love of technology. I enjoyed the hands-on work in the laboratory which solidified my path into engineering. From high school, I received my bachelor's degrees in electrical and computer engineering; the first dual degree from Northeastern University. I consulted for the U.S. Federal Government defense department writing and testing software. Soon after I started my first company performing systems integration of large-scale networks. At the time what we designed, implemented, and managed required security to be an integral part of the network. This was the beginning of my career in cybersecurity.

*What are the main challenges you've encountered as a woman in cyber security, and how did you overcome them?*

Starting during my schooling and early career, I was a minority as a woman. At the time, women made up less than 10% of technical studies and careers. When I started consulting and later in my businesses, I encountered even less women. Many times, I was the only one in the room. Confident in my abilities, I learned to be polite, but definitive when I wrote opinions, worked on projects, wrote reports, and presented materials at large conferences. Having self-assurance and learning which battles were worth fighting, taught me that it is better to win the war, then small battles.

*What are the things you've learned being a woman in the cyber security industry?*

It can be very lonely at times. Being a small part of the workforce makes it difficult to have peers like yourself. This requires developing soft skills and needing to feel like you must be smarter than everyone else. It is necessary to know and be confident in your abilities, but you need to be open to different ideas, ways of doing things, ands working with others.

It's crucial to keep up with learning new technologies and methods. As technology morphs at such as fast rate, failure to keep abreast of the changes will quickly make you obsolete. Take time for training. Many companies require training to be done on your own time, but it is worthwhile to do so. Not only does it open up more opportunities, it opens the door for more financial renumeration.

Get a mentor or two. It doesn't need to be a woman, but you need to have someone to assist you in your career journey. Look for people you consider a role model that has significantly more experience than you think you need and communicate with them. Tell them you admire what they have accomplished and that you are looking for someone to be your mentor. You'll be surprised at the positive response you get. Once you have a mentor, use them! Schedule calls with them at least once a quarter. Put together an agenda for every meeting. Be proactive for yourself, but also remember to keep up with what your mentor is doing. Congratulate them on their successes and ask questions about their work.

*What advice would you give to women who would like to join the cyber security industry?*

Remain confident in your abilities. You want to be in cybersecurity for a reason, so trust your talents and build upon your strengths. Take as many opportunities as possible to work on new projects, represent the company at conferences, write articles, and keep on learning. The more you know and are willing to share, the more likely you will be selected to rise the corporate ladder.

*What role does diversity play in cyber security?*

Diversity is key to team development and growth. It is proven that diverse teams perform better than non-diverse teams. The differences in approaches, experiences, and viewpoints bring a robust solution to all team members. Diversity leads to more innovation that find unique solutions to complex problems. Understanding different points of view opens yourself up to new ways of approaching the same problem. Specifically in cybersecurity, someone from a dissimilar background than you will attack the problem differently. By learning these tactics, you add invaluable tools to your toolbox.

*It is widely known that cyber security is still a very male dominated industry, even though it is 2024. Why do you think there are so few women in cyber security?*

While many women participate in STEM programs starting in elementary school, they find less of themselves as their education grows. By the time college graduation comes, women are exposed to a scarcity of other women in the marketplace. This is part of the fact that some women choose not to enter the field, but it also comes from the lack of focus on certifications and hands-on work experience. Taking the college path provides strong critical thinking skills that are necessary throughout a career, but without hands-on experience, many employers do not want to take a chance on entry level cybersecurity professionals. Obtaining certifications during college can help alleviate some of the experience issues, but does not substitute for actual hands-on experience. Participating in summer internships and experiential learning programs assist in bridging the experience gap. The key is to get your foot in the door. Once in the workforce, seek out organizations such as Women in Cybersecurity (WiCyS) to network with other women. Mentor junior women while you, yourself are being mentored. Remember, what goes around, comes around.

*Who are your role models in cyber security?*

Jane Frankland is a cybersecurity business owner who has worked diligently to expand the pie for women in cybersecurity. She has been involved in cybersecurity as an employee, owner, author, and speaker. Her book INSecurity focuses on the lack of women in the cybersecurity field. She is a role model in that she "walks the talk."

Stacey Champagne is the Founder and CEO of Hacker in Heels. Hacker in Heels supports women in cybersecurity in their quest to excel in their chosen field. Her Changemaker program also supports women who are looking to break into cybersecurity. Her advocacy for women has inspired more women to enter the cybersecurity field.

Jen Easterly, the Director of the Cybersecurity and Infrastructure Security Agency (CISA) plays a critical role in safeguarding the United States. From her start in the military, she has amassed significant experience that she leveraged into the corporate world and then back to the U.S. Government. As she garnered progressively more power it increased her ability to affect security policy. Although she plays a major role at CISA, she still finds time to give back to the community.

*If you could go back in time to your first days in the industry, what would you do differently or tell yourself?*

Be more confident. Being an introvert, I was always working with little socializing. When I did socialize, it was with my peers as opposed to my managers. While this helped me become more extroverted, it didn't expose me to educating my managers on my importance to my projects and my contributions. By communicating with my managers, I would have had the opportunities for positional and monetary compensations at a higher level than I received. Take the time to talk with your manager, not just about the project, but what your goals and aspirations are. This will assist them in looking for ways to promote you in areas you are interested in.

*If you could give women considering a career in cybersecurity one piece of advice, what would it be?*

Be confident in your capabilities and never stop learning.

*And finally, tell us a few fun things about yourself! Do you have an unusual hobby for example, or a fun fact about yourself that you can share?*

I used to race cars. I enjoy Formula1 which led me to take a competitive driving course. From there, I drove various sports cars on road tracks.

# Drenusha Salihu

**Job Title:** Cyber Security Professional & Founder

**Company/Organisation:** CANCOM/Women4Cyber Kosovo

*Tell us a bit about your background, your career to date and what you currently do in cyber security.*

My journey is a dynamic blend of technical development and advocacy. I am currently a vital member of a specialized team within a SOC department where I am deeply involved in addressing day-to-day security challenges and leading initiatives to maintain and fortify the infrastructure crucial to SOC operations. My career trajectory began over four years ago, working with servers, core banking systems, databases, and other important components of IT. It was a foundational period where I built my technical skills and developed a deep understanding of IT operations before transitioning to a focus on IT security. This transition has allowed me to continue engaging in hands-on technical work, with a primary emphasis on security-related responsibilities.

Beyond the confines of my technical domain, I wear another hat (not the black hat) but that of the Founder of Women4Cyber Kosovo. Here, my mission transcends the technical world as I work to bridge the gender gap in cybersecurity, a global issue. As part of this, I was honored with the European Cyber Woman Hope medal in December 2023. Through initiatives and programs designed to empower women, I advocate for diversity and inclusivity in an industry often resistant to change. From sharing insights in public speaking engagements to facilitating workshops and training sessions, I strive to empower women to navigate the digital landscape with confidence and resilience.

*How did you get into the field of cyber security?*

The path to my career in cybersecurity began with a childhood filled with virtual adventures and hours spent playing video games. From a young age, I was captivated by the endless possibilities of technology, and it became clear to me that my future would inevitably be intertwined with the world of tech. Despite occasional temptations to pursue other paths, such as becoming a pilot, my passion for technology always remained.

As I grew older, my fascination with technology also grew, but so did my awareness of its darker side. I began to see how technology could be used not only for innovation and progress but also for malicious purposes. It was a realization that ignited a sense of responsibility within me. I couldn't simply stand by and watch as individuals could so easily fall victim to cyber threats and attacks. This understanding led me on a journey of discovery. I started learning about cybersecurity, eagerly absorbing everything I could about hackers, cyber threats, and security measures. It was during this time that I got introduced to the terms "hacker" and "cybersecurity," sparking a curiosity that would shape my future.

Wanting to also learn professionally, I embarked on a journey that would lead me to the doors of an extraordinary institution in Prishtina known as the "Cyber Academy." It was here that I had my first direct encounter with the fascinating world of cybersecurity. Through hands-on experiences and exposure to topics like penetration testing, I delved into the intricate world of digital security with enthusiasm and determination.

The Cyber Academy became the catalyst for my transformation from a tech enthusiast to a cybersecurity professional. It was a place where my passion for technology found purpose, and where I discovered my calling in protecting digital landscapes and ensuring the security of online spaces. As I reflect on my journey, I am filled with gratitude for the experiences and opportunities that have shaped my path in this field. From the virtual landscapes of my childhood to the immersive learning environment of the Cyber Academy, every step of my journey has been guided by curiosity, passion, and a relentless pursuit of knowledge. And now, as I continue to grow in this field, I am inspired by the belief that my work is not just a career, but a mission to contribute to protecting the digital world for generations to come.

*What are the main challenges you've encountered as a*

*woman in cyber security, and how did you overcome them?*

In my journey as a woman in cybersecurity, I've encountered the pervasive challenges of gender bias and stereotypes. Often, in team meetings, my insights would be dismissed while my male counterparts would be praised for similar ideas. Despite possessing equal expertise and qualifications, there lingered an unspoken assumption that my gender somehow diminished my capabilities. To overcome these obstacles, I adopted a proactive approach. I made a point to assert myself confidently, ensuring that my voice was heard and my contributions were valued.Building strong relationships with colleagues, seeking continuous feedback, and investing in professional development became integral parts of my strategy. Moreover, I embraced the role of an advocate for diversity and inclusion, championing initiatives to address biases and foster a more equitable workplace. Through my dedication, I navigated the landscape of gender bias, ultimately earning recognition based on merit and expertise rather than stereotypes.

Another point is that of under-representation of women in cybersecurity, which is a significant challenge that hits close to home for me. It's disheartening to see so few women in the field, whether it's at industry events, in leadership roles, or even among my peers. This lack of representation not only makes it harder for women to break into the industry but also deprives us of diverse perspectives and role models to look up to.

*What are the things you've learned being a woman in the cyber security industry?*

Reflecting on my journey as a woman in the cybersecurity industry, I've gleaned profound insights that have shaped my professional and personal growth. Firstly, I've learned the power of resilience. Despite encountering numerous obstacles and biases along the way, I've developed a resilience that enables me to persevere and thrive in the face of adversity.

Moreover, being a woman in cybersecurity has taught me the importance of assertiveness. I've learned to confidently assert myself and advocate for my ideas, ensuring that my voice is heard and my contributions recognized in professional settings. This assertiveness has been instrumental in overcoming challenges and making a meaningful impact in the industry.

Furthermore, I've come to appreciate the value of networking. Building and nurturing professional relationships has not only opened doors to new opportunities but has also provided invaluable support and mentorship throughout my career journey.

Additionally, continuous learning has been a cornerstone of my growth in cybersecurity. The field is constantly evolving, and I've embraced a mindset of lifelong learning to stay abreast of the latest developments and technologies.

Finally, my experiences as a woman in cybersecurity have fueled my passion for advocacy. I'm deeply committed to championing diversity and inclusion within the industry, advocating for underrepresented voices, and driving positive change

*What advice would you give to women who would like to join the cyber security industry?*

First and foremost, let your passion for cybersecurity be your guiding light. It's the fuel that will keep you motivated through the ups and downs of your journey. Continuously sharpen your skills and knowledge, seizing every opportunity to learn and grow in this rapidly evolving landscape. Seek out mentors and allies who can provide valuable insights and support as you navigate your career path. And remember, confidence is key. Believe in yourself and your abilities, and don't hesitate to advocate for your worth in professional settings. Embrace diversity and resilience as your allies, knowing they'll serve you well as you tackle the challenges and seize the opportunities that come your way. With determination, support, and a sprinkle of positivity, there's no limit to what you can achieve in the dynamic world of cybersecurity.

*What role does diversity play in cyber security?*

Diversity isn't just a catchphrase in cybersecurity, it's the lifeblood of our industry. From a professional standpoint, diversity brings a wealth of perspectives, experiences, and fresh ideas to the table, enriching our problem-solving capabilities and driving innovation. When we embrace diverse voices and backgrounds, we're better equipped to tackle the toughest challenges head-on, finding creative solutions that we might never have considered otherwise. What's more, diversity makes us more resilient in the face of an ever-changing threat landscape, helping us adapt and respond quickly to new risks. But beyond the professional benefits, diversity also fosters a sense of inclusivity and belonging, ensuring that everyone, regardless of background, feels valued and empowered in our cybersecurity community. By celebrating diversity, we not only strengthen our defenses against cyber threats but also create a more welcoming and supportive environment for all of us to thrive.

*It is widely known that cyber security is still a very male dominated industry, even though it is 2024. Why do you think there are so few women in cyber security?*

I've seen first-hand how the cybersecurity world often feels like a boys' club, and it's disheartening. The truth is, there are a bunch of reasons why women aren't as visible in this field. For one, there's this long-standing idea that cybersecurity is just for guys, which can really put off women from even considering it as a career option. Plus, when you look around for role models or mentors who look like you, they're pretty scarce. It's tough to see yourself succeeding in a field where you don't see anyone who looks like you doing it.

Then there are these sneaky biases in hiring and promotions that can make it feel like the odds are stacked against us. And let's not forget about workplace cultures that aren't always welcoming or inclusive. When you're up against all that, it's no wonder that some women might think twice about diving into cybersecurity.

But here's the thing: we've got to change that narrative. We need to break down those barriers, challenge those stereotypes, and make sure that women know they belong in this field just as much as anyone else. That means giving them the support and encouragement they need to pursue careers in cybersecurity, offering up mentorship opportunities, and creating workplaces where everyone feels valued and respected.

When we do that, we're not just helping out women professionals, we're strengthening the whole cybersecurity and IT industry. After all, diversity isn't just a buzzword, it's the secret sauce that makes us better at what we do. And the more diverse our workforce, the stronger and more resilient we'll be in the face of whatever challenges come our way

*Who are your role models in cyber security?*

My role models in cybersecurity are those heroines whose names might not grace magazine covers or conference panels. They're the ones who quietly work behind the scenes, diligently protecting our digital world from threats big and small. They're the mentors who patiently guide newcomers through the complexities of the field, the innovators who fearlessly push the boundaries of what's possible, and the advocates who tirelessly champion diversity and inclusion. While their names might not be widely recognized, their impact on the cybersecurity community is immeasurable, and they inspire me every day to strive for excellence and make a difference in my own wa

*If you could go back in time to your first days in the industry, what would you do differently or tell yourself?*

If I could turn back the clock to my early days, I would offer myself some heartfelt advice infused with the wisdom gained through experience. Firstly, I would remind myself to embrace the learning curve with patience and humility. Cybersecurity is quick evolving field, and it's okay not to have all the answers from day one. Instead of feeling overwhelmed by the complexities, I would encourage myself to approach each challenge as an opportunity to learn and grow.

Secondly, I would emphasize the importance of building a strong professional network and seeking out mentorship early on. Connecting with cyber professionals and learning from their insights and experiences can be invaluable in navigating the nuances of the industry and accelerating career progression.

Lastly, I would remind myself to prioritize self-care and maintain a healthy work-life balance. This field can be so demanding and fast, but it's essential to make time for relaxation, hobbies, and personal relationships to avoid burnout and sustain long-term success

*If you could give women considering a career in cybersecurity one piece of advice, what would it be?*

If I could share one piece of advice with women considering a career in cybersecurity, it would be this: believe in yourself. The cybersecurity field can be daunting, I know. It has its complex challenges and as mentioned before it's a rapidly evolving field. But don't let that intimidate you. Trust in your abilities and your capacity to learn and adapt. You have unique talents and perspectives to bring to the table, and the industry needs more diverse voices like yours. Don't be afraid to express yourself, speak up, and advocate for your ideas. You've got this.

*And finally, tell us a few fun things about yourself! Do you have an unusual hobby for example, or a fun fact about yourself that you can share?*

When I'm not involved in the world of cybersecurity, you might find me exploring the great outdoors. I have a deep passion for hiking, and there's nothing quite like disconnecting from technology and reconnecting with nature. It gives me a sense of peace and renewal, reminding me how essential it is to find balance in life.

I'm also a big fan of mystery novels. There's just something about immersing myself in a good mystery and trying to piece together the puzzle alongside the characters that I find so enjoyable. It's my favorite way to relax and escape from the stresses of work.

I'm a bit of a foodie and enjoy experimenting with new recipes in the kitchen. Cooking has always been a creative outlet for me, and there's something incredibly satisfying about bringing together different flavors and ingredients to create a delicious meal.

So, whether I'm hiking a mountain, unraveling a mystery, or whipping up a culinary masterpiece, I'm always eager to dive into new experiences and embrace the joy that life has to offer

# Caitlin Sauza

**Job Title**: Program Lead, Training Delivery

**Company/Organisation:** Cybermerc Pty. Ltd.

*Tell us a bit about your background, your career to date and what you currently do in cyber security.*

My background in cyber security so far has been brief, but jam-packed. I 'officially' started my career in September 2022 as a Graduate Cyber Security Consultant – focusing on the Governance, Risk & Compliance (GRC) space. In July 2023, I transitioned into a new role at a different company, as Program Lead, Training Delivery – where I managed our commercial Training portfolio. Most recently, in February 2024, I made an internal move within the organisation, taking on the position of Project Manager, where I now focus on managing company-wide Cyber Security projects with distinct objectives, timelines, and deliverables. While some may perceive frequent role changes as daunting, I view my dynamic career path as a continuous upward trajectory, presenting opportunities for growth, new challenges, and the chance to refine and expand my skills.

*How did you get into the field of cyber security?*

My career trajectory of Getting Into Cyber Security has been non-linear, to say the least. Initially, I chose the traditional route of going to university immediately after graduating high school – ultimately accomplishing a Bachelor of Cyber Security with Distinction from Deakin University. But, taking a few steps back, I had doubts during my degree – choosing to take a year off of study to pursue other interests. In that time I held three different positions in the community services sector. I even entertained the idea of not completing my degree. I learned that what made me happy was giving back to others. Ultimately, and realistically, I only had one year left of my degree – so I was going to finish it, and that I did! In May 2022, my partner and I moved to a different state, which would be the perfect opportunity for me to begin looking for my first full-time role in cyber security. I knew that I would not land a job in the timeframe I had set myself (three to six months) if I simply applied to countless job advertisements and hoped for the best. What I did do however is network my butt off, online and in-person – setting myself apart from the competitive climate that is landing an entry-level cyber security position. I ended up getting an offer in the aforementioned role as a Graduate Cyber Security Consultant (in the fourth month of my search). I did not attend a sin-

gle networking event the year following that offer (haha)
– socialising is draining for an introvert.

*What are the main challenges you've encountered as a
woman in cyber security, and how did you overcome them?*

Personally, the professional development aspect has been
the most challenging part. Being a woman in cyber security, the imposter syndrome is real. Little did I know, I
would end up passing the Certified Information Security
Manager (CISM) exam just 8 months into my career. Prior
to starting my first role, I knew professional development
and lifelong learning was key in cyber security – so I ended
up discovering this new initiative called the Tangible Uplift Program (TUP). The goal of the Program is "...start a
national movement of tangible uplift to careers of women
in cyber security." From then, I was hooked. I became a
part of a tribe of women who support each other in their
achievements and empower one another to succeed. If not
for that program I would not have passed the exam in that
timeframe, and I would not have put myself forward for my
next challenge, of five upcoming technical cyber security
trainings. Build that tribe and believe in your abilities.

*What are the things you've learned being a woman in the
cyber security industry?*

If you are open to it, and willing, you can learn just about
anything on the job and even succeed your mentors in the
process. Be a go-getter.

*What advice would you give to women who would like to
join the cyber security industry?*

Network, network, network! This 'tip' which was instilled
into us at university, in truth, actually works. Each of

my jobs have come from making connections, maintaining them, and seeking guidance when in need.

*What role does diversity play in cyber security?*

In my current role, plenty. Having two men as bosses, they look to me for a different perspective, and readily listen and take action based on my own thoughts and opinions, and the consensus of the team. Don't underestimate that comment you have in your mind at your weekly stand-up, it might change the trajectory of the entire project.

*It is widely known that cyber security is still a very male dominated industry, even though it is 2024. Why do you think there are so few women in cyber security?*

As mentioned earlier, there is that inherent imposter syndrome. Additionally, it is believed that men take more chances and opportunities than women do in their careers. We need to build our confidence by building that professional and support network around us, and keep progressing in our careers.

*Who are your role models in cyber security?*

Oh gosh, I've got an entire knowledge base section dedicated just to this question – I couldn't pick just a few: `bit.ly/top-cyber-security-voices`.

*If you could go back in time to your first days in the industry, what would you do differently or tell yourself?*

Take the time to research the company that you are potentially getting an offer from. Speak to current and former employees, seek our reviews in any form possible. This will enable you to make informed decisions based on fact.

*If you could give women considering a career in cyberse-
curity one piece of advice, what would it be?*

Don't stop learning. If you are like me, you're not naturally
inclined towards reading books, that's perfectly fine. There
are so many different resources out there for you to be
able to empower and advance your career. Don't listen to
those who doubt you. You don't have to have a degree,
what matters is your willingness to put in the effort and
demonstrate that you are deserving of the role through
hard work and dedication.

*And finally, tell us a few fun things about yourself! Do you
have an unusual hobby for example, or a fun fact about
yourself that you can share?*

Well, to my partner's delight, I've recently become very
keen on playing golf – I think I'll be just as good as him
soon! I also have a Corgi named Alfie, who is my fur baby.

# Shifali Sharma

**Job Title:** Cyber Security Analyst

**Company/Organisation:** Infosys

*Tell us a bit about your background, your career to date and what you currently do in cyber security.*

I basically came to Australia from India to pursue MS degree and a dash of international allure led me to the land of kangaroos and Vegemite. As soon as I finished my masters, I faced real challenges to get my first break in IT as I was just a temporary resident in Australia. Luckily, stars aligned and i got selected in BMW Head office to work as a technical intern. Can you believe it? I was rubbing virtual shoulders with business big shots from Germany to

227

South Africa in Australia. Fast forward to the next chapter: Infosys rolled out the red carpet, and suddenly, I found myself knee-deep in cyber shenanigans at NBN which was a huge win for me as I gained so much hands-on experience on different cyber security tools to work on.

*How did you get into the field of cyber security?*

A curious girl with a knack for adventure and a love for puzzles. I found my way into the thrilling world of cybersecurity like it was a secret garden waiting to be explored. Cybersecurity felt like the perfect fit – a blend of challenge and excitement. So, here I am, breaking stereotypes and navigating the digital landscape with a smile on my face. Because in this cyber journey, every challenge is just another chance to show that girls can rock the tech world too!

*What are the main challenges you've encountered as a woman in cyber security, and how did you overcome them?*

Being a woman in cybersecurity brought its own set of challenges, but I approached them with resilience and a sprinkle of positivity. Whether it was tackling the gender gap or handling occasional skepticism, I found strength in embracing my unique perspective. By showcasing my skills with confidence and leaning on the incredible support of fellow women in the field, I turned challenges into stepping stones for growth. Together, we're rewriting the script, creating a more inclusive and empowering space within the cyber world. #CyberWomenRise

*What are the things you've learned being a woman in the cyber security industry?*

I embraced each challenge as a chance to showcase my skills

and uniqueness. Armed with confidence, a supportive net-work, and a dash of resilience, I turned those challenges into stepping stones. The camaraderie among women in cybersecurity has been like a secret sauce, making the jour-ney not just about overcoming obstacles but also building a more inclusive and empowering space for everyone. #Cy-berSheroes

*What advice would you give to women who would like to join the cyber security industry?*

To all the incredible women eyeing the cyber realm, my advice is simple: Dive in fearlessly! Embrace your unique perspective and skills, and don't be daunted by the stereo-types. Seek out mentors, join supportive communities, and trust in your capabilities. The cybersecurity field is vast, and your diverse talents are not only welcome but crucial. Let your passion guide you, stay curious, and remember, you have a community of cyber-sisters cheering you on.

*What role does diversity play in cyber security?*

Diversity is the heartbeat of cybersecurity, infusing it with a tapestry of perspectives, skills, and innovative solutions. In this ever-evolving landscape, having a diverse team is like wielding a superpower against the dynamic threats we face. Different backgrounds and experiences bring unique insights, challenging the status quo and enhancing our ability to adapt.

*It is widely known that cyber security is still a very male dominated industry, even though it is 2024. Why do you think there are so few women in cyber security?*

The gender gap in cybersecurity persists, and while progress has been made, challenges linger. Factors like societal stereotypes, early educational biases, and lack of visible role models can discourage women from entering the field. It's crucial to debunk the myth that cybersecurity is solely a male domain and highlight the diverse skill set women bring. By fostering inclusive educational environments, promoting inspiring female leaders, and challenging stereotypes, we can encourage more women to join the ranks of cyber defenders, creating a stronger and more representative industry for the future. #WomenInCyber #TechEquality

*Who are your role models in cyber security?*

I'm inspired by figures like Brian Krebs, whose investigative journalism sheds light on cyber threats, and Parisa Tabriz, the "Security Princess" at Google, for her dedication to a safer online space and advocacy for diversity. Their passion, expertise, and positive impact make them standout role models in the ever-evolving world of cybersecurity

*If you could go back in time to your first days in the industry, what would you do differently or tell yourself?*

Remember to embrace the learning process and don't be afraid to ask questions. Cherish every challenge as an opportunity to grow and expand your knowledge. Build strong connections with peers and mentors, for the cybersecurity community is incredibly supportive. And most importantly, never underestimate the power of curiosity and continuous learning – it's the key to staying ahead in this dynamic field. You've got this!

*If you could give women considering a career in cybersecurity one piece of advice, what would it be?*

Dear Future Cybersecurity Trailblazers, my advice to you is to embrace your unique perspective and skills. Your diversity strengthens the industry, bringing fresh ideas and approaches. Don't hesitate to be confident in your abilities, seek mentorship, and contribute your voice to the cybersecurity community.

*And finally, tell us a few fun things about yourself! Do you have an unusual hobby for example, or a fun fact about yourself that you can share?*

Here's a heart-warming fun fact about me as a girl in tech – I once believed that technology wasn't my calling, doubting whether I could ever find my place in the IT world. But guess what? Life had a delightful twist in store! Today, not only am I thriving in the tech space, but I've also become a source of inspiration for other amazing women who, just like me, once questioned their tech journey.

# Dr Carrine Teoh Chooi Shi

**Job Title:** President (Cyber Security and Governance)

**Company/Organisation:** ASEAN CIO Association

*Tell us a bit about your background, your career to date and what you currently do in cyber security.*

Tell us a bit about your background, your career to date and what you currently do in cyber security. I have over 15 years of experience in cybersecurity field, even at the era when cybersecurity was at infancy, I worked for Government linked agency in the field of cybersecurity. The areas of cybersecurity which I worked on was CNII protection, personal data protection, privacy, standards and cybersecurity frameworks and policy.

*How did you get into the field of cyber security?*

I was in Electrical & Electronics Engineering field before I ventured into the field of cybersecurity. I was trained and grow on the job in cybersecurity. My CEO believed my EE engineering background Is adaptable in the field of cybersecurity. He was right, and I enjoyed the work and challenges in cybersecurity.

*What are the main challenges you've encountered as a woman in cyber security, and how did you overcome them?*

The main problem was the perception that woman in cybersecurity lacked skills and knowledge. I gained my knowledge and enhanced my skills in the field in order to strengthen my position and reliability. I also took cybersecurity certifications such as CISSP and CBCP, and the exams and knowledge with addition of the experience qualified my CISSP and CBCP.

*What are the things you've learned being a woman in the cyber security industry?*

Women in cybersecurity are capable and knowledgeable. We shld be in position to demonstrate more of our strength and expertise. As a woman in Cybersecurity, with experience and knowledge, we should set example and work as role model and mentor for the new women professionals in cybersecurity.

*What advice would you give to women who would like to join the cyber security industry?*

Take up the challenge at work. Know your stuff, learn and read up on the trends and new skills. We also need to connect more with other women in the industry, to support and encourage each other.

*What role does diversity play in cyber security?*

Diversity gives us more creative and impactful solutions in cybersecurity. The trends and growth in cybersecurity field is never linear, it can be exponential and disruptive. We need diversity in talents and thinking methods for us to address these changes.

*Who are your role models in cyber security?*

I look into the moving trends in cybersecurity, especially in ASEAN region. The ASEAN region is fast moving and hungry for digitalising, with the support of governments and private sectors, Cybersecurity field is growing fast and the need of strategic and overview of ASEAN cybersecurity is paramount. I also hope to encourage more women in cybersecurity in the region, by providing support and motivations.

*If you could go back in time to your first days in the industry, what would you do differently or tell yourself?*

Never try never know. Always willing to take the chance and learn. It is also important to learn from the industry peers and colleagues in the field.

*If you could give women considering a career in cybersecurity one piece of advice, what would it be?*

Never stop learning and always support each other.

*And finally, tell us a few fun things about yourself! Do you have an unusual hobby for example, or a fun fact about yourself that you can share?*

I'm an active yoga practitioner and looking forward to running a half marathon this year.

# Charlotte Smith

**Job Title:** Skills Growth Lead

**Company/Organisation:** CyNam

*Tell us a bit about your background, your career to date and what you currently do in cyber security.*

Attended university began career in Retail Management in London hit at 21 as far as a female could go in the late 80's went back to complete Post Grad CIPD. Began a career in HR promoted to Regional Health and Safety Manager for a major food retailer then entered Recruitment. I set up 2 recruitment agencies. Had 3 girls, was single mum working all the way through and began working in higher education/ business development. I then moved to larger colleges, focussing on new sectors and building industry engagement relations, started to work for a new concept

'Business Development Centres in the Midlands and then as the Cyber Quarter (Midlands Centre for CS) came to life I transferred across because I understood how business worked I built relationships and I then I during Covid I organised the CyberQuarter Fringe Festival and met Lisa :)!!

Cyber became a big thing and here I am.

Working for CyNam as Skills Growth Lead and Cyberfirst Regional Manager for the SW and its just the best. Partnering Academia, Industry and Govt. Its different every day and there is just not enough time to get everything done that we need to.

*How did you get into the field of cyber security?*

I am a relationship builder. I find what a business needs, wants, what is of benefit to their bottom line and I take a genuine interest in them and bring them with me on a journey and I collaborate always

Phishing and being safe online was a huge problem no one understood it so I built a programme and introduced it to SMEs to enable them to work safer better and feel more confident.

*What are the main challenges you've encountered as a woman in cyber security, and how did you overcome them?*

I have not had many challenges to be honest connected with the tech side only in communication perhaps where I don't speak the Tech language too much and so I need to ask for more information and perhaps due to the nature of the people in those roles asking for more detail doesn't always come with a smile

I have worked with a couple of patronising academia who thought 'age' an issue as well as being female; these you are never going to change their outlook but being a success in a new role makes them sometimes realise what might have been, and I always think look where you are now so it's very satisfying

I do though work a lot with other women which has been great because in this sector there is no bitchiness about capability or position it is always hard earned from everyone so there is always a lot of mutual respect.

*What are the things you've learned being a woman in the cyber security industry?*

It is 100

However the importance of language and non verbal communication and the art of building long lasting genuine relationships is also key.

*What advice would you give to women who would like to join the cyber security industry?*

Just do it !!

Explore all the positives of your personality and creativeness because there are roles out there available for everyone and the more adaptable you are the more worth you have.

And make sure your always think outside the box, build relationships and develop communication skills is key to success You are capable, strong, able to multi task, and you can do the job not just think you can do the job and tell people how adaptable to a role you are.

*What role does diversity play in cyber security?*

Enabling the industry to compliment society especially as it delves into replicating and completing tasks done by others is key and to reflect that society too is utmost.

It is important that products are fit for market and can be used by all who are well able and less.

Face recognition recognises all creeds colours race and sex and age.

*It is widely known that cyber security is still a very male dominated industry, even though it is 2024. Why do you think there are so few women in cyber security?*

I am always chuckling at this as I work mainly with just women so it's bizarre.

I think a lot of women are in the industry they just don't feel the need to shout about it they're too busy doing the job and maybe don't feel the need to go shout about it.

But looking at key people in roles of leadership so many are women now that I worry we might be just on the edge of fighting for equality and it starting to be rebuffed because we need to be inclusive.

Girls I work with in schools and colleges however cannot see the fun element of the industry and the expertise required because companies do not think to explain their roles in practical ways something.

I am determined to change to ensure that everyone understands what a Scrum master does for example.

Organisations also do not see how important it is to have a good mix of employees and that all add into the mix of a being part of a great company reflecting different views.

*Who are your role models in cyber security?*

Mads Howard

Lindy Cameron

*If you could go back in time to your first days in the industry, what would you do differently or tell yourself?*

I would perhaps try to do more online courses to back up my knowledge and to just feel more confident, but I was asked to enter this sector because of my previous knowledge and expertise that the sector needed to work with and adapt, so don't entertain the Imposter Syndrome, enjoy that you are an expert in your own field and god look at you now. :)

*If you could give women considering a career in cybersecurity one piece of advice, what would it be?*

You are amazing, you have already had to work twice as hard as any bloke, you are here full of competence and capability, you have the world at your feet and the ability to communicate and work with many different types of people because of the natural skills you have; which are to be determined, efficient, be able to multi task, and read the room and dress unbelievably, enjoy that you are female and use your own USP to your advantage because believe me so will others who are not so well placed as you.

*And finally, tell us a few fun things about yourself! Do you have an unusual hobby for example, or a fun fact about yourself that you can share?*

I'm a Grandma, who thought a grannie would be doing Cyber. I pinch myself every day that I have found a job and a team that are amazing and I think it shows, and that it shows that people are what makes 'amazing' happen. :)

# Rebecca Taylor

**Job Title:** Threat Intelligence Knowledge Manager

**Company/Organisation:** Secureworks

*Tell us a bit about your background, your career to date and what you currently do in cyber security.*

When finished at the University of Portsmouth back in 2012 with my English and Creative Writing degree, I wasn't sure what to do next or where to turn. I was working in White Goods Insurance when I was headhunted for a Personal Assistant role at Secureworks.

On joining Secureworks I instantly saw the depth and breadth of opportunity for me in cyber. My initial role was focussed on supporting the EMEA Managing Director, helping him keep on top of his diary, organising travel and meeting rooms. But through this I was exposed to so many areas of the business, so many thought leaders and role varieties, but all held by people from different background with different skillsets. This inspired me and helped me see that I too could have a role in cybersecurity, but that had to be driven by me and my aspirations. So I begun to study cyber topics that inspired me, explored what really made me tick, got myself a mentor and held on for the ride!

I moved from the Personal Assistant role, into Change Management and Coordination. This role was focussed around business process and the project management of adversarial and Incident Response efforts. From here I moved into Incident Command as their first Knowledge Manager. This role was a real thrill but was not for the faint-hearted! I worked across 50 major customer incidents in 18 months, from ransomware to denial-of-service attacks. The hours were long, the knowledge gathered was interesting and at times overwhelming, but it was a role where I truly evolved and was able to make significant organisational changes and improvements to our data collect, processes and procedures. This was also where the importance of inclusion really started to glare into my role - The fact I was working with such a diverse group of individuals across the world on what was often their worst day, all with their own styles, backgrounds, belief systems, neurodiversity and potential adjustments. It was more important than ever that everyone was able to bring their full selves to 'the fight' and so I was really able to embrace accommodations and normalising the 'diversity chat' into my role.

I then was offered the chance of a lifetime, to join the Secureworks Counter Threat Unit™ (CTU). Since I begun in the organisation, the CTU had always been a pipe dream, a 'I could never do that'. But I can honestly say my tenacity, openness to learn and talk to anyone, and willingness to help, got me there more than any technical qualification or IT skillset. I leapt at the chance and so now have been Secureworks first Threat Intelligence Knowledge Manager for 18 months.

My role is 'all things knowledge'- You can think about that from a threat intelligence perspective as anything that pertains to our intelligence gathering and understanding of 'the threat'. I ensure we are ingesting, standardising, verifying and publishing critical indicators and intelligence. I am focussed heavily on ensuring our intelligence as well as supporting processes and procedures are searchable and accessible to the varying teams, tools and community members who require such important information. It is a role which brings me a lot of joy, allows me to learn consistently, but changes every single day - I am always on my toes. It is also the first role where I think I have been able to bring my entire authentic self to. My leader lets me do my thing, inspires me to work hard, but completely appreciates I am a female, a Mother and Wife, so the juggle for me is very real.

*How did you get into the field of cyber security?*

I got my first job in Cyber Security after being headhunted for a Personal Assistant role. But I *really* got into the field when I took up my next role as a Change Manager and Coordinator. This was the role where I really begun to understand the needs and concerns of organisations from a cybersecurity perspective, ranging from compliancy checks, to red-teaming, to threat hunting, to compromised networks and beyond. It was my first role directly communicating with customers during their time of need, and inspired me to think 'What could I do more to help'. But it was also the role where I started to feel my own knowledge gap, that I didn't necessarily know all the lingo and what different exercises or attacks meant. So this was also the point where I begun to dig deep and study so I could truly understand the field and what part I wanted to play in it.

*What are the main challenges you've encountered as a woman in cyber security, and how did you overcome them?*

Still to this day, I struggle regularly with self-doubt. I have always been someone who wants to jump in and support, but always questioned 'Am I the right person?' and 'Can I do this?'. I'm not sure where it comes from but I do know I am someone who needs reassurance and affirmation to know I am pleasing my leaders and organisation. As I said, this is still something I feel to this day, but I am embracing it and have spun the self-doubt to actually be that I care deeply for what I am doing, that the concerns and nervousness is just because I simply care that much. That helps me feel more at ease with it all.

The second challenge has really been more focussed around my personal identity. I started in industry as a 24 year old single woman who was just living for the moment. Since then I found my husband, got married, had two children, all of which have affected my identity and what I want from my life. This really hit home for me after having my daughter, as I left as one person, and came back 6 months later as an entirely different human being. I had new expectations, new worries, new traumas, had to figure out what my life looked like now as a working Mum and someone accountable for a teeny weeny person's survival! The only way I found to find peace was just to be totally honest with people I trusted. I spoke to my Leader, I talked things through with my mentor, I even got myself a Counsellor. If my support network didn't know what was going through my mind and that I was struggling, how could I expect them to be having my back and helping me? Although it can be hard to lay it all out there, 'a shared problem, is a problem halved'.

*What are the things you've learned being a woman in the cyber security industry?*

I have learnt that whilst my own organisation has my back as a female, and has a variety of policies, support mechanisms and opportunities to help me specifically as a woman in tech, a lot of organisations just don't and subsequently a lot of women are infact alone. According to ONS, 'An estimated 17,000 women left the UK tech industry between Q4 of 2022 and Q1 of 2023, with a further 3,000 leaving before Q2'. When we drill that down that is roughly 110 a day. How can this be happening?

So the core thing I have learnt is the importance of resource groups, events and support groups to bring women in cyber security together, so no-one has to be alone. We have to pull together, we have to advocate for each other, and we have to be the voices that encourage other females to join us in industry. If we do this, then maybe one day we won't be the only woman in the room in our cybersecurity organisations, and maybe just maybe there will be a whole board of women running a cybersecurity firm! We can live in hope right!

*What advice would you give to women who would like to join the cyber security industry?*

You can do it! There is a space for you. It can be hard when you look at a cyber security organisation but cannot see anyone like you and so therefore aren't sure to apply. But the fact is in industry we are there and we see you and we want you!

My second piece of advice is to not be hung up on the need to be technical. Yes there are roles which require technical skillsets, but cybersecurity isn't all coding and hacking. As long as you are keen to learn and ultimately want to help keep people safe, then there can be a place for you in Cyber Security.

*What role does diversity play in cyber security?*

Diversity is not just a buzzword but rather a crucial component that strengthens the cybersecurity field. Embracing diversity leads to more effective problem-solving, innovation, and decision-making processes, while bridging the skills gap and fostering cultural understanding. If cybersecurity organisations prioritise diversity and inclusion, we can all build an aligned cybersecurity ecosystem that reflects the diverse nature of our society and better protects our digital world.

It is imperative for organisations to actively promote and create an inclusive environment that welcomes individuals from all backgrounds. By doing so, we can create a more secure and resilient cybersecurity landscape that benefits us all. When we consider cybersecurity, this understanding and embracing of diversity can truly transform our ability to predict, understand and deter adversaries, and better enable us to defend our teams, communities and even our countries.

*It is widely known that cyber security is still a very male dominated industry, even though it is 2024. Why do you think there are so few women in cyber security?*

I think as an industry we have had a real push in recent

years on attracting female talent to work in cybersecurity.
There are lots of events, more work within Universities,
lots of career fairs, fabulous work by charities and organisations like TechSheCan and CyberFirst. I think the real
issue is in the retention once a female is working in a cybersecurity role. If ONS are to be believed, and 17000 women
are leaving the cybersecurity industry a year, then something is fundamentally wrong.

I think leadership and industry need to ask the real question to their female counterparts and employees - What do
Women want? Women are driven by different objectives,
different limitations, different aspirations to men, yet the
industry is framed around males. If we go down the route of
health and wellbeing, women have many significant health
hurdles including periods, fertility experiences including
endometriosis and IVF, pregnancy as a whole and even
menopause to contend with, which affect their ability to
flourish and maybe even work in a field that can be incredibly fast paced and male led. These topics alone can
be hard to bring to the male-dominated table.

I think if we can get a better grip on what matters to
women in industry, make authentic and progressive change
to our organisational policies, role opportunities, even pay
structures to better empower our female colleagues, industry would likely see a lot more women sticking around!

*Who are your role models in cyber security?*

I have been incredibly fortunate to know many amazing
individuals in cyber security so this is quite a challenging
question! Soon as this is 'The Rise of Cyber Women' it
feels right to sing the praises of two amazing women in
industry who have fundamentally changed my life.

My first and biggest role model is my friend and super-
woman in cyber Emma Jones. Emma worked at Secureworks in Incident Response and was the first person to
really make me feel brave enough to advocate for DE&I
change. She would give anyone the time and space to talk,
she challenged the status quo, she was a subject matter
expert in Incident Response, she was making waves in industry to advocate for all underrepresented groups to have
voices and platforms. She now works for CrowdStrike as
a Principal Consultant in their Cyber Incident Response
and Readiness team and my goodness are they lucky! She
is just fabulous in every possible way.

It would be entirely wrong of me to write this piece if
I didn't call out my CEO Wendy Thomas. Wendy is a
gamechanger and gives me hope. Wendy leads our organisation, has worked incredibly hard to get to where she is,
has had lots of experiences across the industry, and has
done all this as a Mother and a Wife. She is also very nor-
mal (which might seem like an unusual thing to say), but
she is always open to a catch up, cares about our fam-
ilies and has actually on several occasions advocated for
me (which has also blown my mind!). I see myself in her,
and I see that if I keep trying my best I can be a successful women in cyber too. The day she became CEO I
cried, because it meant change had happened and that she
was not only a positive role model for me, but for women
everywhere.

*If you could go back in time to your first days in the in-
dustry, what would you do differently or tell yourself?*

You don't have to be technical! You offer more than that!

Joining as Personal Assistant it was hard at points to
think I could do more than book meeting rooms and order

lunches. But is was positive leadership, pushing myself and digging deep that got me to where I am today. I am not from a technical background and I don't need to be. Cyber Security isn't all about being 'technical' as that diversity of thought and experience is what helps us keep the bad guys at bay!

*If you could give women considering a career in cybersecurity one piece of advice, what would it be?*

Get yourself a mentor! Mentors are sounding boards, perspective providers, connectors of dots and networking advocates. There are many charities and organisations out there that offer industry mentoring, which can be invaluable if you are considering a role or a pathway.

I have always had mentors, both internal and external to my organisation, and I would have been entirely lost without them.

*And finally, tell us a few fun things about yourself! Do you have an unusual hobby for example, or a fun fact about yourself that you can share?*

I am very music orientated, and a huge lover of all things theatre. My favourite production is Dear Evan Hansen! I have now made my daughter a theatre-buff and so we are exploring the West End together to find new shows and experiences.

# Andrea Themistou

**Job Title:** Associate Director (Cyber Security & Digital Identity)

**Company/Organisation:** Protiviti

*Tell us a bit about your background, your career to date and what you currently do in cyber security.*

I am originally from Cyprus and I moved to the London for my studies. I studied MEng Computing at Imperial College London, I then worked for some time as software developer in various companies and eventually joined Deloitte's Cyber Risk Services team. That's when I got into Identity & Access Management area of Cyber Security that I have been focusing for more than 10 years. I joined Protiviti 4 years ago as technical leader / SME in the UK Digital Identity team.

*How did you get into the field of cyber security?*

When I was choosing my university courses, I was still unsure whether to go with Maths that I always loved or try to enter the technology world which wasn't a natural choice for women at the time so I applied for both courses at various universities. When I got an offer from Imperial College in London to study Computing, I decided to give it a go, knowing that it's not going to be easy. I got into Cyber Security during my last year at university and I did my year end dissertation on "Multiparty session types", which are used to describe the communication between multiple participants by ensuring the security of the communication. At that time, I was even considering doing a PhD at on cyber security, but in the end, I decided to go to the industry and started applying for graduate programmes on Cyber Security that would provide me both the necessary training and work experience.

*What are the main challenges you've encountered as a woman in cyber security, and how did you overcome them?*

My initial challenge was actually getting a job! Coming from a foreign country, with English not being my first language and also being an introvert, I found it difficult to perform in the interviews. Although I had the skills, I was scared and wasn't coming across as confident. So, I had to go through many interviews even though I had a good CV. The turning point was when I finally decided what I wanted to do; I wanted to become a cyber security professional. Whilst looking for a job, I have started studying on my own for the Certified Information Systems Auditor (CISA) certification and kept practicing a lot for interview questions to build the confidence I needed to get through the interview stages and get the job.

The main challenge for me on the day-to-day job is that I am not the stereotypical technical resource. As women we have to fight with the unconscious bias as people won't think that you may be the most technical person in the room or have the deepest expertise. I would many times have to work outside my comfort zone and try to overcompensate on discussions to change the mindset.

*What are the things you've learned being a woman in the cyber security industry?*

There is definitely a place for women in Cyber security and there are opportunities for us to have a successful career. However, most of us still get imposter syndrome especially when being in an environment where we are a minority. We feel that we may not be good enough and start challenging ourselves. I learnt that I needed to find my own path and not try to copy anyone else's career, follow my passion and the rest will fall into place. I learnt to believe in myself and if I am ever in a toxic environment, still do my best to complete my job but then get out. It is also very important to have advisors and internal sponsors that are supportive, believe in you and become your advocates.

*What advice would you give to women who would like to join the cyber security industry?*

Be yourselves and believe in your abilities. Working in a male oriented environment, might make some women feel uncomfortable and start challenging their capabilities. Find your passion, spend some time to understand your strengths, focus on improving and demonstrating your skills and don't try to mimic the career path and behaviour of others.

Cyber security is a fast moving environment, where we need to be up to date with the latest technologies. Getting relevant certifications is a way to boost your credibility and industry conferences can give you an understanding of the market trends. Additionally, when working on cyber projects, you can expect to deal with deep technical experts and also business leaders so it is important to build your communication skills and adapt your style and presentation according to your audience.

*What role does diversity play in cyber security?*

I believe diversity of people and skills is very important in any team and environment. When someone hears "cyber", they typically think of people with hoodies coding in a basement. However, it requires a lot more broad skills to have a successful team in any cyber delivery programme. You would encounter roles such as business analyst or project manager, which do not necessarily require deep technical understanding or coding skills but are equally important to the success of a project. Diversity of background and gender also helps with providing a different perspective and generating more innovative ideas.

*Who are your role models in cyber security?*

I've been lucky to meet some great people in cyber security area which have been supporting me through my career. One of them is Roland Carandang who's been leading our Technology Consulting practice at Protiviti and has been a great technical role model for me. What I admire about Roland is his deep expertise in the security domain, he is always up to date with the latest technologies, he finds time to be very hands-on and pursue his passion on security architecture even though he is now one of our global leaders. He is also a big advocate of innovation and always encourages the generation of new ideas and applying those in our work for clients.

*If you could go back in time to your first days in the industry, what would you do differently or tell yourself?*

I would tell myself to be more confident, don't be afraid to pursue a new challenge or make mistakes as this would give a great learning experience to further develop myself

*And finally, tell us a few fun things about yourself! Do you have an unusual hobby for example, or a fun fact about yourself that you can share?*

Having a lot of extra time during covid, I have got into crocheting. I love making amigurumi (crochet stuffed animals), which fills my creative nature and is a new challenge every time. It also helps me relax in the evening after a long day and it's also a great gift for my friends and family.

# Eleanor (Ellie) Upson

**Job Title:** Managing Director

**Company/Organisation:** Hawksvale Insights

*Tell us a bit about your background, your career to date and what you currently do in cyber security.*

I have worked in the Cyber Security space for over 10 years now – which seems to have flown by. I initially started my career as a general cyber security practitioner before specialising into Cyber Threat Intelligence. I was a CTI manager for a big-4 consultancy for several years, delivering CTI managed services into global organisations as well as supporting the delivery of red team engagements.

I am now the MD for a boutique cyber threat intelli-

gence company which I established last year and remain a
CREST-certified Threat Intelligence Manager and through
which I provide CTI and cyber security support to growing businesses. I also facilitate threat intelligence training
which I love doing!

*How did you get into the field of cyber security?*

I studied Medicine at University and took a role as a Junior
Doctor in 2011 – before very quickly realising it wasn't
the job for me. This left me in something of a quandry as
they don't really prepare you for having another career at
medical school, it's pretty much expected that you'll follow
the typical route into the NHS.

As a result I applied for several graduate roles in what
was then called 'information security' and took a role at
a big-4 consultancy in the information security practice.
I wasn't sure what area I would end up in, but while between projects I was asked to cover the holiday of someone
working in the CTI team. I fell in love with the job and
ended up not leaving when they came back from their trip
– I haven't looked back since.

*What are the main challenges you've encountered as a
woman in cyber security, and how did you overcome them?*

I consider myself really lucky in the career I have had to
date, and the supportive companies and colleagues I have
worked for and with.

I struggled with depression in the early years of my career
which I thought was going to result in me leaving the job
I loved. Luckily, I had a superb manager who encouraged
me to be honest about the struggles I was having and
supported me in seeking help. This allowed me to remain

in my role and has led me to be much more open as I've taken on more senior roles.

Balance as a working mother is always going to be a challenge, wherever you are – you feel like you should probably be somewhere else. Now, as I run my own business, I am working hard to embrace flexible working and set clear boundaries. If I can deliver work remotely and be at home when my children get home from school then that's what I do. I am transparent about my need to balance family life and many of my clients have met one of my children through video calls at some point or another. COVID made that much more 'the norm' and in some ways, I am proud that my children get to see me spending time with them, but also running a business. I don't always get it right, the mum-guilt and the work-guilt are still very real, but I am getting better at disconnecting from work when needed.

*What are the things you've learned being a woman in the cyber security industry?*

To appreciate that sometimes I bring a different perspective to a situation. To have confidence in my expertise even if I am the only woman in the room (which does still happen!). That some of the greatest advocates and supporters of women in this career have been some of my male colleagues, who haven't necessarily had the experience of – for example – being the only woman in the room, but who have appreciated those challenges exist and have worked to reduce them.

What advice would you give to women who would like to join the cyber security industry?

*What advice would you give to women who would like to join the cyber security industry?*

Cyber is not just for people who love coding and technology and computers. For every one of them there is another who works on education of people, or processes, or communication and all those roles are equally important.

*What role does diversity play in cyber security?*

Diversity is key across all of cyber but especially within my specialist area of CTI. We have to be able to analyse and evaluate the behaviour of unknown threats and the best way to do that is with a diverse team who bring a range of perspectives, experiences and ideas. If we were all the same, we would be incredibly ineffective!

*It is widely known that cyber security is still a very male dominated industry, even though it is 2024. Why do you think there are so few women in cyber security?*

Perception and portrayal in the media. If you see 'cyber' on TV its all bits and bytes, coding and deploying new tech – very often done by men. You never see anyone going "We need to liaise with HR and write an effective Acceptable Use Policy", so I think many people are unaware of the range of roles, and therefore can't see themselves in that space. It's a job that lots of people still don't understand fully (my family have no idea what I do – especially my Mum!) and if they don't see people 'like themselves' in a role, they don't realise that there is a role there for them.

*Who are your role models in cyber security?*

There are lots of people I admire in Cyber Security and if I start naming them I'll miss someone and that will be bad! I was hugely inspired by Nicola Whiting when I saw her speak a couple of years ago. Some of the other independent cyber practitioners I work with especially Rob McBride and Martyn Gill have supported me and driven me to be better and I really appreciate that – I hope to be able to emulate them and their business and management skills in the years to come!

*If you could go back in time to your first days in the industry, what would you do differently or tell yourself?*

Don't try to pursue what you think you "should be" doing to be more "cyber" (I tried to learn to code and hated it). Hone the skills you already have – there is almost certainly a place for them within the field.

*If you could give women considering a career in cybersecurity one piece of advice, what would it be?*

Talk to people about their roles – there are so many different ones! Ask people what they love about what they do and find the thing that makes going to work a pleasure rather than a chore! Also there is often flexibility to move around in this space, if you don't like what you are doing, try something new!

*And finally, tell us a few fun things about yourself! Do you have an unusual hobby for example, or a fun fact about yourself that you can share?*

I collect and build Lego models and am currently building a massive model of Hogwarts because I also love Harry Potter. I knit very slowly and not very well. I have just set up a Twitter account that shares a fact a day about birds, because birds are great!

# Ismini Vasileiou

**Job Title:** Associate Professor and Director of the East Midlands Cyber Security Cluster

**Company/Organisation:** De Montfort University and East Midlands Cyber Security Cluster

*Tell us a bit about your background, your career to date and what you currently do in cyber security.*

With a foundation in computer science stemming from my undergraduate degree, I embarked on a diverse academic journey that eventually led me to complete a professional doctorate in Education. Since 2005, I've been immersed in academia, exploring various roles within university settings, broadening my understanding of educational systems and methodologies. As an established academic in the field of computer science, I've delved deeply into Cyber Education and Human factors, recognising the pivotal role they play in cybersecurity. Recently, I've taken on the initiative of founding and leading the East Midlands Cyber Security Cluster, a proactive effort aimed at fostering collaboration and cohesion within the region's cybersecurity landscape. Through this role, I strive to amalgamate expertise, drive innovation, and reinforce the cybersecurity infrastructure of the East Midlands, contributing to

265

the collective resilience against cyber threats.

*How did you get into the field of cyber security?*

While teaching a diverse curriculum spanning computer science and specialising in database development, I gradually realised the increasing importance of cybersecurity principles in our digital landscape. It became evident that understanding cybersecurity was paramount to comprehending the intricate workings of computer systems. My line manager, recognising the intersection of my expertise in computer science and the emerging field of cybersecurity, emphasised the significance of addressing human factors within this domain. Initially, I was hesitant to pivot my focus entirely, reluctant to delve into a new area of expertise. However, after a wager that perhaps tested my skepticism, I found myself drawn into the world of cybersecurity. Embracing the challenge, I dedicated myself to expanding my research and understanding in this field. This newfound passion and expertise eventually led to an invitation from DSIT to lead and facilitate the development of the East Midlands Cyber Cluster, an opportunity that further solidified my commitment to advancing cybersecurity initiatives in the region.

*What are the main challenges you've encountered as a woman in cyber security, and how did you overcome them?*

Navigating an academic career in cybersecurity as a woman, particularly within a predominantly male environment, has often felt like a lonely journey. The academic landscape can be isolating, especially when faced with gender disparities and limited support structures. At the outset of my career, I also went through a divorce and took on the sole responsibility of raising my two children. Balancing the demands of academia with the responsibilities of single parenthood added another

layer of complexity. Raising children as a single parent can undoubtedly hinder career progression, as the juggling act of fulfilling academic duties while attending to family needs can be overwhelming. The lack of adequate support mechanisms further exacerbates the challenges, leaving little room for personal growth and professional advancement.

I found strength and motivation through various projects focused on Equity, Diversity, and Inclusion (EDI) that I led, including the successful leadership of the Athena Swan award. These initiatives not only raised awareness and enhanced the working environment but also provided support to other colleagues.

Those experiences kept me motivated, gave me strength, and empowered me to challenge perceptions and break stereotypes.

*What are the things you've learned being a woman in the cyber security industry?*

As a woman in the cybersecurity industry, I've learned several valuable lessons that have shaped my journey. Firstly, I've realised the importance of resilience and perseverance in overcoming gender biases and stereotypes that may exist within the field. I've learned the significance of advocating for diversity and inclusion, not only to create a more equitable work environment but also to foster innovation and creativity within teams. I've discovered the power of mentorship and networking, as building connections with other women in cybersecurity and that has provided me with valuable support and insights throughout my career. Very importantly, I've learned to embrace challenges as opportunities for growth and to continually push boundaries to achieve success in a male-dominated industry.

Finally. . . . . I have learned the importance of being unapologetic in asserting my expertise, ideas, and contributions within the cybersecurity industry. Recognising my worth and refusing to diminish my achievements or capabilities due to societal expectations has been crucial in navigating professional challenges and demanding respect in male-dominated spaces. Being unapologetic means owning my accomplishments, speaking up for myself and others, and advocating for equitable opportunities and recognition, regardless of gender. It's about embracing confidence in my abilities and refusing to conform to traditional norms that may undermine my value as a woman in cybersecurity.

*What advice would you give to women who would like to join the cyber security industry?*

- Build a Strong Support Network: Seek out mentors, allies, and networks of women in cybersecurity. Surrounding yourself with supportive individuals can provide guidance, encouragement, and valuable insights as you navigate your career.

- Cultivate Resilience: Understand that the cybersecurity field may present challenges, including gender biases and stereotypes. Cultivate resilience to overcome obstacles, learn from setbacks, and use them as opportunities for personal and professional growth.

- Embrace Continuous Learning: Cybersecurity is a dynamic field with ever-evolving technologies and threats. Stay abreast of industry trends, acquire new skills, and pursue continuous learning through training programs, certifications, and networking events.

- Be Unapologetic: Own your accomplishments and don't hesitate to assert your expertise. Be unapologetic in promoting yourself, your skills, and your contributions. Confidence and self-advocacy are crucial in breaking barriers and gaining recognition.

- Advocate for Inclusion: Actively support and promote diversity and inclusion within the industry. Encourage organisations to implement inclusive policies, challenge biases, and contribute to creating environments where everyone's talents are recognised and valued.

- Seek Opportunities to Lead: Look for opportunities to take on leadership roles, whether within projects, initiatives, or industry organisations. Leadership experience not only enhances your skills but also contributes to breaking gender stereotypes.

- Network and Collaborate: Build relationships with professionals in the cybersecurity community. Networking provides avenues for mentorship, collaboration, and exposure to diverse perspectives, which can be instrumental in your career development.

- Find Your Niche: Cybersecurity is a vast field with various specialties. Identify your interests and strengths, and explore niche areas where you can make a unique impact. Specialising in a specific area can set you apart and enhance your career trajectory.

Remember, your unique perspective and contributions as a woman in cybersecurity are invaluable. By embracing these principles, you can not only thrive in the industry but also contribute to its evolution towards greater diversity and inclusivity.

*What role does diversity play in cyber security?*

- Enhanced Problem Solving: Diverse teams bring together individuals with varied perspectives, experiences, and backgrounds. This diversity of thought enhances problem-solving capabilities, allowing for a more comprehensive and innovative approach to addressing complex cybersecurity challenges.

- Improved Decision-Making: Inclusive teams foster a range of viewpoints, leading to more well-rounded and informed decision-making processes. Considering diverse perspectives helps anticipate and mitigate potential risks more effectively, reducing vulnerabilities in cybersecurity strategies.

- Increased Creativity and Innovation: Different backgrounds and experiences contribute to a creative and innovative environment. Cybersecurity requires constant adaptation to evolving threats, and diverse teams are better equipped to generate novel solutions and stay ahead of emerging risks.

- Better Understanding of User Behaviour: Cybersecurity is not solely about technology; it also involves understanding human behaviour. Diverse teams, especially those including experts in psychology and human factors, can provide valuable insights into user behaviours and motivations, improving the design of security measures and education programs.

- Broader Skill Sets: A diverse workforce brings a wide range of skills and expertise. Cybersecurity encompasses various disciplines, from technical expertise to legal and policy considerations. Having a diverse team ensures a broad spectrum of skills necessary to address the multifaceted nature of cybersecurity.

- Enhanced Global Perspective: Cyber threats are not confined to a specific region or demographic. A diverse workforce reflects a global perspective, helping organisations understand and defend against threats that may originate from different parts of the world. This is particularly important in today's interconnected digital landscape.

- Increased Representation: Having diverse professionals in the cybersecurity field promotes representation and inclusivity. This, in turn, encourages more individuals from underrepresented groups to pursue careers in cybersecurity, contributing to a positive feedback loop that strengthens the overall talent pool.

- Cultural Competence: In a globalised world, understanding diverse cultures is essential for effective cybersecurity. Cyber attackers often exploit cultural nuances in their tactics. Having a diverse team can help organisations better navigate and understand these cultural intricacies, improving security measures.

Diversity in cybersecurity is not just a matter of fairness; it is a strategic imperative that directly contributes to the effectiveness, adaptability, and resilience of cybersecurity efforts in an ever-

evolving digital landscape.

*It is widely known that cyber security is still a very male dominated industry, even though it is 2024. Why do you think there are so few women in cyber security?*

The underrepresentation of women in cybersecurity persists despite significant efforts to address gender disparities in the field.

- Perception and Stereotypes: The perception of cybersecurity as a male-dominated, technical, and inherently masculine field persists, discouraging women from pursuing careers in cybersecurity. Stereotypes about women's abilities in STEM fields may also discourage them from considering cybersecurity as a viable career option.

- Lack of Role Models and Mentorship: The scarcity of visible female role models and mentors in cybersecurity can hinder women's entry and progression in the field. Without relatable role models to emulate or mentors to guide them, women may feel isolated and unsupported in their cybersecurity pursuits.

- Unconscious Bias and Discrimination: Unconscious bias and discriminatory practices in hiring, promotion, and workplace culture create barriers for women in cybersecurity. Biased perceptions of women's technical abilities, leadership potential, and suitability for cybersecurity roles perpetuate inequalities and hinder women's advancement in the field.

- Workplace Culture and Environment: Hostile or male-dominated workplace cultures in cybersecurity organisations can alienate women and contribute to their underrepresentation. The prevalence of toxic work environments, harassment, and lack of inclusivity can drive women away from pursuing or remaining in cybersecurity careers.

- Educational Pipeline Challenges: Gender disparities in STEM education and training programs contribute to the underrepresentation of women in cybersecurity. Limited access to quality STEM education, lack of encouragement and support for girls and women in STEM fields, and systemic barriers in educational pathways impede women's entry into cybersecurity roles.

- Work-Life Balance Challenges: The demanding nature of cybersecurity roles, characterised by long hours, high-stress environments, and on-call responsibilities, can pose challenges for women seeking to balance their professional and personal lives. The lack of supportive policies and accommodations for work-life balance further exacerbates these challenges.

Addressing the underrepresentation of women in cybersecurity requires concerted efforts to dismantle systemic barriers, promote inclusivity, and foster supportive environments where women can thrive. Initiatives focused on promoting diversity and inclusion, expanding access to STEM education and training opportunities for women, challenging stereotypes, providing mentorship and sponsorship programs, and advocating for equitable policies and workplace practices are essential for creating a more gender-balanced cybersecurity workforce.

*Who are your role models in cyber security?*

While I don't have specific role models in cybersecurity, there are several individuals whose work and contributions I greatly admire. For example, I hold immense respect for well-known professors and researchers who have made significant strides in advancing cybersecurity knowledge and education. Their dedication to expanding our understanding of cybersecurity concepts and their commitment to mentoring future generations of professionals inspire me. While I may not have direct mentorship from these individuals, their work serves as a source of motivation and guidance as I navigate my own path in the cybersecurity field. Additionally, I find inspiration in the collective efforts of diverse professionals who collaborate to address cybersecurity challenges and promote inclusivity within the industry. I draw inspiration from the collective expertise and passion of those committed to making meaningful contributions to cybersecurity.

*If you could go back in time to your first days in the industry, what would you do differently or tell yourself?*

- Seek Mentorship and Guidance: I would encourage myself to actively seek mentorship and guidance from experienced professionals in the industry. Building relationships with mentors can provide valuable insights, support, and advice to navigate challenges and make informed career decisions.

- Take Risks and Step Out of Comfort Sones: I would remind myself to embrace opportunities for growth and to step out of my comfort sone. Taking calculated risks, exploring new areas of interest, and pushing boundaries can lead to personal and professional development.

- Stay Resilient and Persistent: I would remind myself to stay resilient and persistent in the face of challenges and setbacks. The journey in cybersecurity may present obstacles and failures, but perseverance and resilience are key to overcoming adversity and achieving long-term success.

- Network and Build Connections: I would encourage myself to network actively and build connections within the industry. Networking provides opportunities for collaboration, knowledge sharing, and professional growth, and can open doors to new opportunities and experiences.

Overall, I would tell myself to approach my journey in the industry with curiosity, adaptability, and a willingness to learn and grow. Each experience, whether positive or challenging, contributes to my development and trajectory in cybersecurity.

*If you could give women considering a career in cybersecurity one piece of advice, what would it be?*

- Embrace your uniqueness and never underestimate your capabilities.

- Believe in yourself, your skills, and your potential to make a meaningful impact in the field.

- Don't let stereotypes or gender biases deter you from pursuing your passion for cybersecurity.

- Be proactive in seeking out opportunities for learning, growth, and advancement.

- Surround yourself with supportive mentors, allies, and networks of women in cybersecurity who can offer guidance, encouragement, and solidarity along the way.

- Remember that your voice, perspective, and contributions are valuable assets to the cybersecurity community.

- Stay resilient, stay determined, and continue to pave the way for greater diversity and inclusion in the field.

*And finally, tell us a few fun things about yourself! Do you have an unusual hobby for example, or a fun fact about yourself that you can share?*

I have a deep fascination for magicians. No matter how hard I try, I can never seem to unravel their tricks, and to this day, my attempts end in failure. The mystery behind their illusions never fails to amuse me. In fact, I recall a memorable incident where a magician had to pause his performance because I couldn't contain my laughter for over ten minutes—much to the amusement of those around me!

https://www.csu.org.uk

Cyber Security Unity is a global community membership organisation and content hub that is dedicated to bringing individuals and organisations together who actively work in cyber security.

Our mission is to foster greater collaboration, industry best practice and information sharing in the cyber security industry to help combat the growing cyber threat.

To find out more and get involved please email info@csu.org.uk for more information.

Security Blend Books is a boutique publisher for the security industry. Working with modern print on demand technology, we provide not only a route to market for new and upcoming security authors, but expert subject matter expertise on the field.

To find out more about us, other upcoming books, and how our submission and editorial process works, go to our website.

https://securityblendbooks.com

Printed in Great Britain
by Amazon

38739818R00165